# WHY WE TALK

## *The Truth Behind Word-of-Mouth*

7 reasons
WHY YOUR CUSTOMERS
will—or will not—
TALK ABOUT YOUR BRAND

Bolivar J. Bueno

CREATIVE CRAYON PUBLISHERS

New York

*Dedicated to marketers and business owners committed to building honest relationships with customers everyday.*

ISBN: 0-9714815-3-9

Creative Crayon Publishers
230 Kings Mall Court, Suite 142
Kingston, New York 12401

Cover art and interior design by Melissa Thornton

Printed in the United States of America

**Albert Einstein** gave his students a test. One student pointed out that the test contained the same questions that had appeared on the test the previous week. Dr. Einstein replied, "Yes, but this week, the answers will be different."

# CONTENTS

# FOREWORD

I suspect that most 13-year-olds are curious about their future—I know I was. One day, my mother brought home a little black and yellow hard-backed book called *Careers* (I'm not entirely sure of the title, as this was nearly 50 years ago). I found a quiet place and devoured the book.

The book covered many career possibilities with a two-or three-page description of each career detailing the skills and education required for it. I skipped most of the chapters after two or three sentences until I got to the chapter on Advertising. I felt like I'd been struck by lightning. The skills required were not only the very things I was interested in, but I was good at them. There was nothing said about math, and that sealed the deal. Any business that used words, pictures and ideas was clearly superior to doing arithmetic forever. This was the career for me.

Thanks to my Mom's gift, I never gave casual or serious thought to what I wanted to be when I grew up. If fact, that career focus influenced the elective courses I took in High School. I chose my minor studies of Psychology and Art well before I registered as a college freshman. When I went to college, I only had one major, and if I could choose my course of study all over again knowing what I know now, I would keep it the same.

After I completed the required course work in Advertising, I began to realize that I didn't know very much, and since it was time for me to get a job, I was horrified by how much I didn't know.

The first half of my career, I became a relentless student of what others in my field said and did. I learned methodologies, processes and measurements from great thinkers and practitioners within the advertising business. It didn't occur to me that if all I did was what everyone else did, I limited my potential to "the norm." Safe, but average. Not a very exciting prescription for business or career success.

As my business responsibilities grew, my bosses continually pointed out that *business outcomes* or *results* always trumped the most sophisticated marketing processes—my safe harbor of "best practices" and advertising measurements were meaningless if I didn't actually grow market share for my company. What good were low-cost CPMs if they didn't build the business?

Only in light of the *expectation of growth and profitability* did I realize what was really important for a marketing executive: Growing the business! Fortunately, what I had studied and learned was useful to my new philosophy, but it was just the beginning of a more rational practice of advertising and marketing.

One of my first steps was to hang a quote by Shakespeare in my office: *What's past is prologue.* What was next was far more important than what I knew, and the process of figuring that out made my career.

I was recruited from Target to be the CMO of Wal-Mart in 1989, a dream job for a marketer. Wal-Mart was firmly focused—obsessed, really—on customers and stressed the importance of respect for the people who came into their stores. That became my bully pulpit.

Of course, expectations for results were intense. I had to figure out how to influence people to choose Wal-Mart more often than our competition. And, believe me, the competition was good.

In this super-charged environment, I realized that to be chosen, we'd better be *worthy* of being chosen: The priorities of our business would have to be the priorities of our existing and potential customers. We had to become an observably-better choice to customers.

I learned that in spite of the "branding" trends, businesses didn't make brands—they made "things" or provided services. Brands were just convenient symbols for people's experiences with those goods and services. If we wanted to have customers for life—not customers for this week's circular—we'd have to do things differently from other marketers, different from conventional wisdom.

We could never tell customers what to think or say. I learned to respect and celebrate those people kind enough to shop in our stores. In fact, I learned to give a voice to the beliefs and experiences of our customers. And I learned that research was really about honestly listening to what customers thought and wanted, and sharing the results with employees of the company so that they felt part of fulfilling the expectations of customers.

This new "against the grain" advertising and marketing strategy changed the way that we did things like buy media, communicate our advertising message and demonstrate our devotion to our customers in our stores.

It was so much simpler than the uber-trendy, *go with the flow*, complex, scientific methodologies that I believed were so important. It required a lot of discipline to disavow the premise that customer-centric marketing was enough. I hung a sign up in my office—something that I wrote for a meeting—to remind me that our customer's priorities, not ours, were most important: *It takes more effort to keep things simple than it does to allow them to become complicated.*

Ten countries and $200 billion later, I was at a meeting of the Retail Advertising and Marketing Association board of directors where we listened to this wonder-kid share some very big and well-articulated ideas about marketing to us over lunch. Though ridiculously young to know the lessons that had taken me most of my career to learn, BJ and I were drawn together in a friendship that has celebrated learning and ideas.

In fact, as I mark five years of retirement from Wal-Mart, I'm pleased to say that BJ and I still make time to share ideas and talk about new life lessons we've learned and how they apply to marketing. You can imagine how pleased I was to get an advanced read of his current big idea, *Why We Talk*. I hope that you'll recognize the truths and wisdom contained in this book. This information will challenge what you believe today and may be hard for you to read. While adopting some of these ideas will be difficult, it will be worthwhile for your enterprise. Whether you're a marketer or a CEO, this book can help you prioritize your go-to-market strategy around what customers want and hopefully, make your business much more talk-worthy.

**PAUL HIGHAM**
Lazy H Ranch | Tusus, New Mexico

# PREFACE:
## BEWARE OF "WOM MARKETERS"

Talk is cheap. Gossip is priceless. And while manipulated talk can be useful if you're selling a film or a novelty that doesn't need any staying power, it's practically worthless if you're hoping to build a brand.

Yet Word-of-Mouth (WOM) Marketing has become all the rage, with "water-cooler talk" becoming a barometer companies use to judge the success of their marketing and advertising campaigns. *What were our numbers yesterday? How can we improve them today? If we can't meet the short-term goals, who cares about the future?* Unfortunately, these companies haven't stopped to consider how driving short-term numbers may be killing their opportunity for long-term success.

Word-of-mouth is like any other form of media. Television is favored for its combination of sight and sound. Billboards are revered for their stopping power, print for its permanency. All forms of media, including word-of-mouth, disseminate information. Word-of-mouth is different from all other forms of media, however, because it is owned by the consumer. They control its content.

Think of it another way: Word-of-mouth is like a pipeline that can carry a variety of things: Gossip; rumor; manipulated talk. It's no different than a pipe's ability to carry drinking water or sewage. You just can't mix the two in the same pipe or thirsty people have a problem. The best and highest use of the word-of-mouth pipe is to allow it to be the people's channel, carrying their gossip and musings. If you pollute the pipe with marketing propaganda, you destroy its purity, and ultimately, its ability to serve your brand long term.

Some word-of-mouth marketers claim you benefit from word-of-mouth during specific windows of opportunity. That's nonsense. Promotions and events have windows; brands have permanence. As long as consumers are benefiting from a relevant experience with the brand, they will talk. Consumers don't need to be given a marketing cue card; they need an environment that allows them to draw their own conclusions and to define their own experience.

The problem with modern marketing is its overwhelming urge to quantify everything. If it can be measured, you can charge for it, and yes, size does matter: The bigger the measurable impact, the larger the monetary compensation for generating the result. The newest playground for metric maniacs is word-of-mouth marketing. The Word-of-Mouth Marketing Association declared in 2005 that it was now using word-of-mouth units to measure the effect of word-of-mouth on ROI. This is further proof that, to its own detriment, marketing has evolved into an industry more focused on making short-term money than on making long-term sense.

Numerous books on poker have been written to teach players the best ways to behave in certain situations, based on available statistics. However, watch any game and you'll see that even experts stray from these rules. Why? Because the players in the game aren't playing statistics, they're playing other people. The best way to play isn't always revealed by statistics.

Statistics give a glimpse of where people are, but they don't tell you where people are going or how they will get there. It's one thing to know what movies are making the most money, but that's not the same as predicting which ones are going to make the most money. If someone could forecast that, the movie studios would be a lot happier.

Look at what's happening: Big brands are paying big money to create "buzz" about their products. These companies then insist they don't pay people to talk, which technically is true—they only give their "buzz" agents free products, coupons, and "points" if they do their homework and report back to the mother ship.

What do you think happens when the buzz campaign ends? Do you really think consumers keep yakking about a product when the incentive to do so disappears? Worse yet, the next product sample shows up in the mail and they're asked to buzz on a new client's behalf. That's not pure word-of-mouth. It's promotion attempting to use word-of-mouth as a media vehicle, which is no different than using radio, television, or direct mail. Ultimately, it runs into a dead end and is enormously risky for companies wanting to build lasting brands.

Promoting products is a totally different discipline than creating brands. True word-of-mouth is totally different than word-of-mouth marketing. *Marketers are in control of communicating a message, but consumers are in control of building brands.*

Word-of-mouth is a single-use medium or a single-use stream, if you will. You can pollute the stream with short-term product promotion or you can leave it for the consumer to use to embrace your brand. It can't be used for both. If you inject your own marketing into the word-of-mouth stream, you pollute its best and highest use—brand building.

Manipulating word-of-mouth to promote a product is like cutting down a forest and using the trees to make paper for millions of flyers that can be passed out to promote saving the trees. Unfortunately, once you've reached millions of people with your *Save the Forest* message, the forest is decimated. We believe that tampering with the natural rhythm of word-of-mouth is dangerous for brands because the best brands are built by true word-of-mouth and gossip.

So pick your poison. If you want to sell product in the short term and aren't worried about building a brand, if you've exhausted every other medium known to mankind, pick up the phone and call any of the self-proclaimed word-of-mouth marketers and buzz practitioners. They've got the metrics on their side.

But be cautioned: Once you pollute the word-of-mouth pipeline, there's no turning back. If you're marketing movies, selling novelties or liquidating books, have at it—these things are not likely to become brands and you will not need the power of word-of-mouth in its purest form. If you are relying on the consumer to turn you into a brand that is embraced by a legion of loyal evangelists, however, don't pollute the best marketing tool ever to roam God's green earth.

**BJ BUENO**
Orlando, Florida

# PART I

## *Overview*

*A summary of what you're about to learn
about the nature of human communication.*

# AN OVERVIEW OF *Why We Talk*

This book is about "why we talk," or more specifically, why your customers talk. For business people, this book highlights the significance of putting your ear to the ground and listening carefully to the whispers of your customers. Listening is your most important discipline if you want to succeed in harnessing word-of-mouth. Management sage Peter Drucker reveals, "The most important thing in communication is hearing what isn't said."

## The Consumer Has Won

Those who still believe you can control the consumer are dead wrong! It's over. Thanks to technology, the consumer has won.

We are living in a Hypersonic Word-of-Mouth World. We are connected in ways that didn't exist a decade ago, or even minutes ago. The rapid advance of technology that allows us to communicate globally has not only shrunk the world, but it has also shrunk our timelines for success or failure. Because of this, we need to look for more relevant answers than we relied on decades ago, last week, or even yesterday.

Much of what we've learned from powerful brands with loyal customers confirms that we must move away from marketing rhetoric and align with people's biologically- and psychologically-rooted unchangeable behaviors. We need to rally around the truth about our customer, not the truth about our product, and certainly not some trademarked process used by marketing practitioners trying to manipulate sales.

*The Power of Cult Branding* reveals that the strongest brands—like Apple, Harley-Davidson, Oprah Winfrey, and Volkswagen—embrace the consumer's control. These brands intuitively know what you hope to learn by reading this book: *Word-of-mouth* can't be created. Instead, we must focus all our energies on creating the stuff consumers will want to talk about. Our job as marketers is to put passion in their hearts by delighting them and fulfilling their needs. We can't put words in their mouths. If we do, they will only spit them out.

The power of the consumer's voice and the power they have to influence others has been greatly amplified by technology (see *Time Compression: The Need for Speed*). The control of your business is now on their lips, not within your corporate towers.

## The Essence of *Why We Talk*

*Talk* is the most powerful media network in the world. It can rescue a dying brand or crash an enormous advertising budget overnight. The power to say something—to express our opinions, to reveal our feelings, and to be heard—is one of the most precious gifts we have.

*We talk because it is our nature to do so. Talking benefits us.* By talking, we can find a banana if we are hungry, or negotiate for love or oil. We talk because it helps us gain what we want.

We talk because we need to be heard. Acceptance of our perspective by others elevates our status and becomes the currency of our own self-worth. Having someone listen affirms our importance.

As humans, we have a biologically- and psychologically-rooted desire to communicate. As the anthropologist Robin Dunbar put it, language enhances our ability to communicate, "to survive in a complex, constantly-changing social world, and to mark other individuals as friend or foe."[1]

## Essential WOM Lessons for All Marketers

*If you truly understand the next 537 words, you're positioned to capitalize on the most powerful communication medium in the world.*

Business is currently recognizing the *effect* of "Word-of-Mouth Marketing," rather than the cause of why consumers talk. Word-of-mouth is organic; it happens on its own. By trying to invent ways to control it, you destroy what makes it special and appealing to people in the first place.

*The important thing to recognize is that you cannot control the consumer's experience, which is what feeds word-of-mouth. When we say brands belong to the consumer, we mean the consumer's experience with the brand IS the brand.*

Understanding trust is key to understanding why word-of-mouth works. Consumers trust each other more than they trust marketers. If we, as marketers, try to manipulate what they say, they will eventually catch on and turn against us. Consumers are in control of this process, not marketers.

What can we take away from this? People will talk without our help. Today, numerous marketing companies promise to generate word-of-mouth, but the idea of hiring "word-of-mouth" is a contradiction. Hiring word-of-mouth goes directly against our nature as human beings. We want to share trustworthy information that makes us important to our group; we don't want to be liars or be manipulated into saying something we don't mean. For this reason, hiring "pretend fans" often backfires. People instinctively want to deal only with companies who have high integrity.[2]

There are no tricks to making people talk. Sure, there are word-of-mouth schemes that use short-term metrics to justify their use, but short-term increases in repeated phrases by consumers are not the true measure of word-of-mouth success. So-called "Word-of-Mouth Marketing" companies often ply consumers with product freebies in order to get them to say positive things about the product. Take away the freebies, and the talk dries up. There is no magic formula to get people to start jumping around and telling the world about a new product or service. *People talk to serve their needs. If telling someone about a new product does not benefit them, they won't talk.*

There are certain biological and psychological needs that make people talk. *If you give someone something to talk about, they will.* That's your job: Create experiences for your customers through your products and services that give them something to talk about. And once they start talking, don't try to manipulate the conversation—sit back, listen, and learn. They will tell you how to create the next thing that will amuse and surprise them and keep them talking.

*The best brand architects create communities not by motivating people, but by building an environment where motivated people are willing to make a maximum contribution.* Psychologist Abraham Maslow had a cautionary question for us all: "Why then do we frequently design organizations to satisfy our need for control and not to maximize the contributions of people?"[3] If today's word-of-mouth marketing practitioners had heeded his warning, they wouldn't have created systems to control the dissemination of information. Information control systems may create good short-term metrics, but ultimately, they can destroy the brand's ability to be embraced by the consumer. (Take the number of weight loss products you've heard about that "guarantee" someone will lose weight, compared to the number of people you know that have actually lost weight using them.)

## The Seven Principles of "Why We Talk" for Marketers

So how do you produce authentic word-of-mouth? You work hard to create amazing experiences for your customers—experiences worth talking about. Here are seven principles to help you better understand your customers' World of Talk:

*1 –*     THE PRINCIPLE OF INTEGRITY:
       THEY KNOW THAT YOU KNOW THAT THEY KNOW

People know you have an intention and that you know that they know you have an intention. What this means from an advertising standpoint is they know you are trying to sell them a product, and they know that you know that they know you're trying to persuade them. Unless you are very adept at meeting their needs, you're going to encounter an impenetrable barrier. Don't think you can deceive them into believing they're not being coerced into buying a product. Even if you think the advertising is solid, they're still going to know. People are much better at detecting deception than they are at being the deceiver.

2 –     **THE PRINCIPLE OF STATUS:**
        **PEOPLE SHARE WHAT MAKES THEM LOOK GOOD**

Both negative and positive information reflects positively on the person conveying the information, as both are useful to decision-making. Negative information is perhaps more useful because it is perceived as being highly diagnostic. Supplying accurate information benefits the conveyer, as it confers status upon the conveyor. Supplying inaccurate information quickly erodes the reputation of the conveyer.

3 –     **THE PRINCIPLE OF COOL:**
        **RIDE IN FRONT OF THE "COOL WAVE" OR WIPE OUT**

In the Hypersonic Word-of-Mouth World, the search for cool is quickly focusing on The Ignored. This means if you see something cool today, you can almost bet it's on its way out and something else will be cool very soon. But remember, in not-too-much-time, that won't be cool either. Pogs—the milkcap game that originated in the 1920s—reemerged and was all the rage in the early '90s, but has now all but disappeared. Technological advances in communication shorten the cycles of "cool." Listen to your customer. In order to be on top, you must know what's cool before it becomes cool. Just like a wave, if you jump too late, you're not going to catch it.

*4 –* THE PRINCIPLE OF GROUPS:
SMALL GROUPS—THE CRITICAL FEW—DICTATE THE LARGE

Customers can be broken down into two subgroups: The trivial many and the critical few. Avoid focusing on the trivial many and find out who comprises your brand's critical few. They are the ones who truly influence their subcultures. The same principle that applies to individuals applies to groups—you need the influence of many small groups to create a movement.

A small group of particular importance is teenagers. Do not ignore them because they don't fall within your target demographic; when you're not looking, they will eat you alive. They are more Internet-savvy than their parents. They know how to access information, and their parents rely on their opinions about purchasing decisions because teens know how to get around on the Internet. In many respects, teens are both the gatekeeper and the bridge to influencing your customer.

*5 –* THE PRINCIPLE OF INFLUENCE:
EVERYONE IS INFLUENTIAL—ESPECIALLY ON THE INTERNET

Connectivity changed the landscape of influence. Everyone is able to influence people in some way, on some subject. No one can affect people's decisions in every category. Those who provide more useful input gain more status, and are more likely to be listened to. Knowledge is power, especially on the Internet, where normal social cues like body expressions and facial reactions are not in place. As a result, anyone can say what he or she is thinking. Comments are judged by their accuracy and value rather than the person's background.

*6 –* THE PRINCIPLE OF MEANING:
PEOPLE TALK ABOUT WHAT'S MEANINGFUL TO THEM

Listen carefully to the critical few to find out what they care about, and give them something to talk about. If you can find ways to amuse them, surprise them, or give them information that will give them esteem among their peers, they will talk. Everyone else will follow.

7 –     THE PRINCIPLE OF SURPRISE:
        PEOPLE LOVE TO SHARE WHAT SURPRISED THEM

Never underestimate the power of surprise. Let the consumer *discover* the best thing about you instead of hearing you shout it from the rooftops.

## How to Read this Book

Throughout this book we will explore several principles of word-of-mouth. We want to get you to think about how you've communicated in the past and how you're going to need to communicate in the future if you want to succeed in the Hypersonic Word-of-Mouth World.

This book is divided into four sections. The first section discusses how today's technologically-driven, hyper-accelerated world is making us talk. We'll explore today's communication landscape, illuminate critical trends, and explore ways this landscape will continue to change to support a customer-driven world.

The second section explores the "meat" of the research on *why* we talk. If you want a deeper understanding of why your customers talk as well as an intriguing scientific look at language and social systems, you'll enjoy this research. We'll also explore historical and anthropological viewpoints, and some psychological disciplines to help you more clearly understand the nature of human communication and how the need to talk relates to your business.

The third section discusses the seven principles all marketers and business owners must understand if they want to increase their chances of stirring positive word-of-mouth. If you're anxious to get into the practical applications of the research, jump right to this section now, and then come back to read the rest of the book.

The fourth and final section summarizes what we've learned and shares insights to help marketers better understand their role in today's Hypersonic Word-of-Mouth World.

These sections do not need to be read in sequence. Feel free to jump ahead to the section that intrigues you the most.

# PART II

## A Hypersonic Word-of-Mouth World

*A discussion of how today's technologically-driven, hyper-accelerated world is affecting the nature of talk. You'll gain a valuable understanding of how the communication landscape has changed and how it will continue to change to support a customer-driven world.*

# THE FORCES BEHIND TALK

You don't need to read this book. You already know why people talk because you already know why you talk—there is no difference. People have talked for thousands of years for the same reasons they talk today. Talking is part of who we are. The infusion of technology into our lives magnifies what we have always done and helps us to do it faster, as if we're "right there" rather than a million miles apart. We can now share our voice, image, and ideas via our virtual presence with tools like e-mail, instant messaging, text messaging, blogs, podcasts, and services like MySpace.com.

A grandmother three states away can view the ultrasound video of the new grandbaby minutes after the image is captured. We are all connected via a plethora of virtual media. Within seconds, the world knows about major events on the other side of the globe, and within minutes the entire office hears about a win, a loss, or an impropriety between co-workers. What is this force that drives us to talk? Why do we do it, and why do we enjoy it so much?

*We talk because it benefits us.* We communicate to acquire the things that make us feel complete. Speaking helps us secure a banana if we are hungry, or negotiate for love or oil. Talking helps us gain what we want.

Our lives revolve around one important concept: *Me.* But that *me* is not alone in the world, that *me* is connected to *you.* We are all storytellers and every story we tell reveals something about our own personal needs. We tell stories and share information because we are the center of our universe. Sitting in a new restaurant, have you ever asked the server, "What do you recommend?" When making plans for Saturday night, have you ever asked a friend, "What movie should I see?" You're not alone. We all rely on the opinions of others to help us make our decisions.

I remember sitting in the theater, watching the previews before the movie began. An eye appeared on the screen for a few moments, staring. Suddenly, the veins popped out and the skin turned green. WOW! It was a teaser for *Hulk*, one of my favorite superheroes. He is the ultimate alter-ego: green and mean, with a dash of compassion. I am an easy sucker for a great adventure story, especially when my favorite hero is the star. There was no doubt: I had to see it. After what seemed like an endless wait, opening night for *Hulk* finally arrived. On my way to the movie, I received a call from a friend in L.A. who had seen it the night before. "How was it?"

"It sucked."

"What?"

"Don't even watch it."

I was dumbfounded. I didn't want to believe that the movie staring my favorite superhero could suck, but I trusted my friend: If he did not like it, the odds were that I would not like it since we have a similar taste in movies. I immediately changed my plans and went to see another movie. Later that evening, I called my brother, who was planning to see the film.

"Salim, I don't think you want to see it. I heard it sucks."

"What?"

"Yeah, Joy and I just watched some chick flick instead."

"That sucks. Hold on a sec bro, I have to text message my friends so we can do something else."

All it took was one friend calling me to stop what I later calculated to be more than twenty people from going to see the movie, and that is only the people I know who were affected directly. Amazing! Little did I realize, we were a small part of a peer-to-peer wave of word-of-mouth that managed to crash the opening weekend of the movie, whose production and marketing budget exceeded $177 million.

It was unexpected. Other studios expected *Hulk* to be such an inevitable success that they chose other weekends to release their films. The massive, unsolicited word-of-mouth campaign fueled by the opinions of disgruntled customers caused *Hulk* to come crashing down 69.7 percent, from $62.1 million the first weekend to $18.8 million the second.[1]

Fans are just as quick to promote a movie as they are to slam it. Amidst negative publicity and studio concerns over a $200 million budget, *Titanic* opened to a mere $28.6 million weekend. The buzz from that weekend, however, was tremendous. In its second weekend, it jumped up by 23.8 percent to $35.4 million.[2] Powered by the overwhelming momentum of pure word-of-mouth, *Titanic* went on to become the number one grossing movie of all time, both domestically and internationally, a record it still holds as of this printing.

In 2005, the movie industry experienced an eighteen-week sales slump from the previous year. Is Hollywood slacking on its productions? Possibly. More likely, it's the result of technology changes like the startling increased use of cell phones, text messaging, and blogging as everyday communication tools in the last five years as we entered the age of the Hypersonic Word-of-Mouth World.

Massive advertising campaigns can no longer mask consumers' opinions. Rick Sands, currently the chief operating officer at MGM, confessed, "In the old days, we used the term 'buying your gross'. You could buy your gross for the weekend and overcome bad word-of-mouth because it took time to trickle out into the general audience. Those days are over. Today, there is no fooling the public."[3] *Buying your gross* translated into deception: Even if consumers hated your product, you could muffle their voices if you spent enough money.

Today, talk is lightening fast, driven by increasingly-efficient communication methods. This presents a difficult challenge to an industry that is relying on an old formula to lead them into the future. A new, connected world is defying the old rules. The most powerful mediums are changing. In 1995, it took three television spots to reach 80 percent of eighteen-to-forty-nine-year-old women. In 2000, it took ninety-seven spots to reach the same number.[4] Screams are heard throughout the business world:

"Mass media is dead and the direct marketing methods are all we have left! Marketing is doomed! We are at the mercy of an angry mob of customers!"

To which we reply, "Get a grip!"

While people have always been vocal about their displeasure, they also are quick to celebrate what they love. Great companies have always listened to their customers, striving to understand and serve their needs, wishes, and desires. The dynamics of a connected world present all of us with an opportunity to truly speak to the customer's needs.

What we are seeing in the world is a leveling of the playing field. Today, companies have to include the customer's in the boardroom and add the consumer's needs to their strategic plans. How can this be a bad thing? A better question is: *What took so long?*

# GRUNT-OF-MOUTH GROWS UP

I bet that a lot of word-of-mouth was generated when the first woman figured out how to start a fire. Imagine the excitement when Ugha called her friends over to show them her creation. Their delight, surprise and intrigue spread "grunts" of Ugha's creation to the rest of her tribe. Grunt-of-mouth was born.

Jump ahead to around 1438 A.D. The Inca's vast communities required a system to convey messages over long distances, so they trained boys from early childhood to become *chasqui*. The *chasqui* relayed messages cross-country. For example, if an army general in Nazca needed to report a village uprising to the Sapa (emperor) Inca in Cuzco, one *chasqui* runner would start from *chasqui* post A in Nazca and run about a kilometer (0.62 miles) to the next *chasqui*, waiting outside another hut at post B. Like a relay race's baton, the message would be propagated using this system over hundreds of miles by hundreds of runners, until the last runner reached the Sapa Inca and delivered the message. In case you are wondering, the messages were delivered word-for-word, without error.

Now take another scenario: August 28, 1844—Fiddler Dick and his gang strike again. They had been robbing people in crowds at railway stations and making their getaway on the train to the next town. Since news of the robbery could not travel faster than a train, they had never been caught. They probably assumed August 28th would end like every other day. What they didn't consider was a new invention called the Telegraph. Once the robbery was discovered, the destination station was telegraphed with the news. When Fiddler Dick got off the train, he was greeted by the sheriff and hauled off to jail. News was traveling faster than anyone could imagine.[1]

Welcome to your lifetime. In the fourth quarter of 2003, Casey Neistat wanted to replace the battery on his Apple iPod. Unbelievably, he discovered that battery replacements were not part of Apple's iPod accessories. Apple suggested he buy a new iPod.

Being a diehard Apple fan, he did, but felt something should be done to change this policy. Casey and his brother Van set out to make a movie to be broadcast over the Internet. The movie showed Casey traveling around New York City spray-painting stenciled text over iPod launch posters: "iPod's Unreplaceable Battery Lasts Only 18 Months." A few days after directing a few friends to their website, they were up to 40,000 hits.[2] By the end of the month, the site had over 1,000,000 hits.[3] Shortly thereafter, Apple introduced a new policy: If your one-year warranty runs out, you can purchase a new battery for $99, or, when buying your iPod, you can purchase an extended warranty for $59.[4] Not bad for a guy that just wanted a battery for his iPod!

Technology has exponentially increased the efficacy of word-of-mouth, helping movies, products, and even political agendas become failures or successes overnight. And if the history of the inventiveness of man is any indication, we've only just begun.

# TIME COMPRESSION:
## THE NEED FOR SPEED

Imagine owning a portable, cordless device that allows you to make phone calls and send e-mails—within seconds. Not impressed? Asking you to imagine this is silly because the odds are you own such a device: your cell phone.

Okay, imagine this same device also allows you to scan barcodes, pay for groceries and subway tickets, operate appliances, serve as your identification, open doors, start your car, and pretty much eliminate the need to carry just about anything else. Now we're talking. The coolest part is…this device is just as real as your PDA.

In the summer of 2004, NTT DoCoMo, Japan's largest cell phone company, introduced this all-purpose cell phone to the Japanese market. Takeshi Natsuno, managing director of i-mode strategy— NTT DoCoMo's wireless net service—describes the company's goal for this phone: "All the credit cards, loyalty cards, keys, money—all that stuff in a woman's purse or a man's wallet—should go into the phone. By having the phone with you, you shouldn't need anything else but your clothes."[1]

Less stuff in my pockets sounds good to me. Carrying a bulky wallet, cell phone, and keys is uncomfortable. Why do I need all this stuff? The car should just open; the cash register should know that it's me. This may sound lazy, but we're always looking for ways to make things a little less cumbersome. After all, a key is simply the solution to protecting and starting our cars. Today, the "key problem" meets a connected world, where my fingerprints can be stored in my mobile device database, relaying my identity. The 21st-Century solution is better, easier, and faster.

*Your Way, Right Away.* Yeah, Burger King got it right back in the '80s. Wal-Mart also understood this, building distribution centers to get customers what they want, when they want it. Awesome. And they delivered on this promise week after week. No wonder they win. Next, Wal-Mart opens the doors 24 hours a day—a killer combination for a world that is ready to get what it wants, when it wants it.

When people went online and started to multitask, keeping up with instant communication became cumbersome. A new, online language quickly entered into the popular lexicon to make communication more efficient. Rather than typing, "That was funny," people began to type, "lol" (short for "laugh out loud"). Four keystrokes replaced fourteen; it was the perfect fix for time-crunched humans.

NTT DoCoMo's phone and this universal language are just two of the thousands of compression ideas responding to our need for speed. We're changing the way we do everything from dating to planning vacations. It used to be fashionable to meet someone at a social event, spend some time with him or her, and then go out on a date. No longer. Speed dating is in. Rather than just meeting one person at a time, you connect with a room full of people, spending less than ten minutes with each person, before you decide who you might like to date.

In the past, the majority of consumers spent months planning their vacations. In 2002, according to the Travel Industry Association of America, "64 percent of U.S. leisure travelers planned at least one of their vacation trips within two weeks of taking that trip."[2]

At the forefront of this hypersonic society are mobile phones and the Internet. Over 2.2 billion people use mobile phones worldwide[3] and, according to the GSM association, a global trade association for mobile phones operators, over 1 trillion text messages are sent each year.[4] There are nearly 1.1 billion Internet connections across the world,[5] and 15.7 billion instant messages are sent each day.[6]

According to Nielsen//NetRatings, teens are spending almost 27 hours a week on the Internet.[67] Jeff Bezos, Amazon.com's CEO, commented, "The rate of change is accelerating: There is more change per unit of time than there was five years ago."[8] The change in technology and people's rate of adaptability is proving hard to predict, as it's exceeding all expectations. In 2003, 22 million homes had high-speed Internet access, twice what was predicted two years before;[9] at the end of 2005, the Federal Communications Commission reported 43 million high-speed residential connections.[10]

While at one time, movies felt major fluctuations in their box-office sales on a weekly basis, now "now, rapid advances of technology, in the hands of an *American Idol* culture quick to express its 'vote 'em off' sentiments, has accelerated the pace of communication so much that Hollywood feels the reverberation at the box office almost immediately."[11] As Reid Rosefelt, president of the movie PR firm *Magic Lantern*, observed, "A guy living in his basement can bring the studios to their knees."[12]

## At The Hand of the Customer …

In case we weren't challenged enough by a world looking for speed, advertisers now compete with time-shifting technology like DVR, where individuals control what they want to see, when they want to see it. Each person is his or her own programmer, able to dictate the perfect viewing experience.

Many want to criticize technology companies and stamp the *Mark of the Beast* on their heads, but these trends were started by consumers and their desire to control their environment rather than technology companies. Without the *need*, there would be no market for the product. It's freaking out the companies who have traditionally owned the distribution channels, and there are movements designed to headlock consumers by "requiring" them to watch advertising or to purchase cable channels they never watch. Good luck with that idea.

Remember what happened when Napster was shut down? Fifty sites offering free music popped up immediately. When those were shut down, another hundred private, untraceable networks were established. The idea of the consumer having so much control is very disconcerting to Big Business. The consumer has become like the card shark: Every time the Establishment develops a new technology to outsmart the shark, the shark finds a way to beat it.

Millions of dollars were spent to prevent CDs from being duplicated. The greatest minds in the industry dedicated countless hours to solving the dilemma. A few days later, a crack was posted on the Internet describing how, for a couple bucks, you could burn as many CDs as you wanted. The solution was simple, but ingenious: Circle the edge of your CD with a black marker to erase the encoding software. Millions of dollars flushed down the drain. Personally, I was impressed.

When Pepsi launched a promotion in conjunction with Apple's iTunes, commercials featured kids who were prosecuted for illegally downloading music. The kids in the commercial claimed they would not stop downloading free music, implicitly referencing Pepsi's promotion that allowed people to download free music if there was a winning number under their bottle cap.

This promotion brought the illegal downloading controversy full circle.

On February 24th, 2004, CNN reported that John Gales, a nineteen-year-old college student, posted instructions on his Website revealing how to look into a Pepsi bottle to determine if it was a winner.[13] The solution was as simple as the CD hack: Tilt the bottle back to see the word "Again" or random numbers. "Again" indicated the bottle was a loser, and the numbers indicated it was a winner.

The iTunes incident mirrors a similar 1992 incident with Topps baseball cards. In every pack of baseball cards, Topps included scratch-off cards in the shape of positions played in a baseball game. If, "by chance," you scratched off the correct spots, you could mail the card to Topps for free Topps Gold Baseball cards. Someone discovered that if you rubbed the scratch-off boxes with your thumb and then held the card up to a light, you could see what was written underneath. At that time, it took about a week for the information to be passed around a group about the size of a small school. By contrast, Gales' site was getting thirty hits per second.

## Biological Need for Speed

This increase in communication efficiency didn't start with our modern, über-connected society. In their book *The Major Transitions in Evolution*, John Maynard Smith and Eörs Szathmáry analyzed the major evolutionary steps, from the evolution of molecules to primate societies developing language, and concluded that all of the transitions were related to a change in the transmission of information.[14] *It might be said, therefore, that increasing the efficiency of transmission is part of a natural, unstoppable biologically-rooted process.*

And we're showing no signs of slowing down. The technological changes in the 1800s equaled the rate of change in the past nine hundred years combined. There was as much change in the first twenty years of the 1900s as there was in all of the 1800s. In the 21st Century, we can expect to see one thousand times more technological growth than we experienced in the 20th Century.[15]

The need for speed is a manifestation of something that is bio-logically rooted in all of us. It's way more significant than cyber-nerds wanting to show off their latest toy with holographic technology.

In response to the technology-driven, overpowering control of the consumer, marketers have responded by attempting to categorize consumer behavior: What people are likely to buy, what categories people are likely to talk about, and with whom. The problem with these studies is they tell us *how* consumers behave, but they fail to reveal the all-important *why*. We must begin to qualify instead of quantify; quantification tells where people are with some possibility of statistical error, but qualification gives insight into how they got there and where they are going.

Time-compression technology has only supported our natural drive to communicate. Like a microphone or amplifier, time-compression technology doesn't change the speaker's voice, it only amplifies it. As Howard Rheingold, a prominent thinker on modern communication and creator of the term "virtual community" observed, when you move discussions online, "The fundamentals of human nature ... always scale up."[16] Simply put, technology provides a superior channel to satisfy our need to be heard. We are talking for the same reasons we have always talked. Technology has only magnified our voices and given them hypersonic speed.

# MEDIA FRAGMENTATION:
## YOU DON'T NEED MASS MEDIA TO
## INSPIRE MASS INTEREST

People don't want to be talked at. People want to be talked with. Media authority Don Tapscott writes, "This shift from broadcast to interactive is the cornerstone of the N-Generation (Net Generation). They want to be users—not just viewers or listeners."[1] This mentality is captured well by one of Tapscott's interviewees in the late 1990s:

> "I love being able to skip all of the fancy advertising if I'm in a hurry," says eighteen-year-old Andy Putschoegl of Oakdale, Minnesota. "I don't have to wait for something to load if I just need to click on a link to another page. I don't even pay attention to the ads on search engines because I'm there for a different purpose—to look information up. If only I could skip commercials on television."[2]

Well Andy, you can skip the commercials, and you should if they don't give you the information you need to make your life better. Despite the screams from industry leaders, Andy is not trying to be mean to marketers or steal money from the hard-working folks in the media. Andy is simply doing what is genetically and biologically rooted in him: He is following the instincts that helped his father's father survive by focusing on those things most likely to increase his happiness. That's great! Way to go, Andy! You represent our most recent evolution, and we agree: "I'm here for a different purpose." Pay attention: His purpose is different from the marketer's purpose. He is looking for something that serves him, and, oftentimes, his needs aren't being served.

This is the consumer's new control: Their way, right away. Andy and his buddies can skip our commercials. Doom for television. Doom for radio. Doom for newspapers. And just wait Cable TV: You too will suffer.

## Ignoring Irrelevance

People have been ignoring bad or irrelevant communication for a long time. Not much has changed. With the remote control's mute button, people can ignore not only what we say, they can silence noise altogether. The decision to not listen, or to channel surf during our discourse on irrelevance, is at their fingertips.

> Do you know that 85 percent of ads *don't* get looked at? … We're not even hated! They ignore us. So the most important thing as far as I'm concerned is to be fresh, to be original—to be able to compete with all the shocking news events in the world today, with all the violence. Because you can have all the right things in an ad, and if nobody is made to stop and listen to you, you've wasted it. And we in America are spending so darn much money for efficiency, to measure things, that we're achieving boredom like we've never achieved it before. We're *right* about everything, but nobody looks.[3]

Those words, spoken decades ago by advertising genius Bill Bernbach, are still relevant to us today. People have always ignored us.

We've moved from a controlled experience—other people tell me what to watch or hear—to I control the experience: My Movies, My Music, and so forth. People have supplanted traditional media for new media. According to comScore Media Metrix, instead of watching television, eighteen-to-thirty-four-year-old males have gone online.[4]

### Category Sites Visited by Males, 18 to 34

| | |
|---|---|
| 71% Pornography | 31% Personals |
| 53% Music | 30% Careers |
| 51% Auctions | 35% Retail – Apparel |
| 48% Sports | 34% Gaming |
| 39% Retail – Consumer Electronics | 32% Movies |
| 38% Automotive | |

The Internet offers the perfect fit for bored young men—a close-to-perfect tool for people who want to be participants rather than observers.

This doesn't mean they are no longer watching television. They are, but an increased number of options has allowed them to hone in on what they really like, moving large viewing audiences to Cartoon Network's *Adult Swim* and Comedy Central. And they're more aware than ever about the products that best fit their lifestyles. How else would they know to buy an iPod?

No matter what their age, people love to be in control of their experience. If two great shows are playing at the same time, you don't have to choose which one you want to watch, or waste time surfing during commercials. Time-saving technologies like DVR allow you to choose what you want to see, when you want to see it. This is what we've always wanted—we can have our cake and eat it too. Bernbach had it right long before DVR or the Internet: *People ignore irrelevant messages.*

## Mass Interest

Nothing has marketing folks more panicked than the fragmentation of media. "Mass media is dead." "The sky is falling." "We're doomed!"

But hold on: Success has never been measured by how much we *utilize* mass media; it's measured by how much interest we can create. Creating mass interest has to do with the message, not the messenger.

In July 2006, network television experienced its lowest ratings in history, beating the previous record set in July 2005.[5] Technology has changed. Media options and consumers have responded. More options allow consumers to migrate directly to their interests.

And it's going beyond television and radio.

The Internet—populated with blogs and podcasts—gives the consumer more objects of desire and distraction. The consumer loves this new media fragmentation, and, as marketers, we've got to find a way to make it good for our brands.

Stop worrying about what's happening to mass media—it was never all it was cracked up to be anyway. Fewer choices made television a passive medium. We tuned in to one of the three networks because that was all there was, and we stayed tuned in because there was nothing else to watch. We didn't pay as much attention to it as the numbers claimed.

Companies that understand their customers embrace fragmentation because it gives them the ability to target a specific message to a specific consumer. More options means people are seeing what they want to see, and fewer people are passively participating in the medium. Since the viewer's participation is active, and they are trying to maximize their time, they are pickier about how long they will watch a program, including commercials. The instant the content seems irrelevant to them, they find the remote or click the mouse.

Consider that the current television advertising market is in the neighborhood of $70 billion, yet more and more people are buying technology to allow them to skip commercials more easily than they did in the past. An analysis of Nielsen data revealed that around 99 percent of people watching top-rated shows on DVR are skipping the ads;[6] over 11 percent of adult households in the United States have DVRs,[7] and the number is rising. Most startling, however, are the results Ephron revealed with their 1999 AdWorks 2 study: *For every dollar spent on television advertising, only 32 cents is returned.*[8]

Benjamin Franklin defined insanity as doing the same thing over and over again, expecting a different result. Throwing more and more money at mass media isn't the answer. Throwing more brainpower at creating mass interest makes more sense. *Give consumers something to remember and they'll talk, whether your media buy is big or small.*

## "Average" Customer = Average Advertising

The problem most companies face is they don't know how to make something interesting. Instead, they try to reach as many people as they can with a mediocre message, hoping what little relevance they have to convey will be interesting to someone. Mass media has always been a game of chance: By targeting the masses, something was bound to stick.

I'm not a big fan of targeting demographics because that strategy typically ignores why people actually respond. Targeting the "average customer" tends to result in average advertising.

Instead of looking at what a customer is (i.e., demographics), it may serve you to look at what they don't have, or, simply, their needs. Psychologist Abraham Maslow accurately described man as a *perpetually wanting animal*, responding more readily to feeling than thinking. Too much of what we throw at our audiences is *observational* instead of *experiential*; as though just because nine out of ten people prefer the product, you should too. I try to impress upon my clients that it is *more valuable to create a brand the critical few can love instead of a brand no one hates.*

## The Opportunity of Fragmentation

The fragmentation of mass media is not a problem; it's an opportunity. Fragmentation creates smaller stages for bigger performances—littler ponds for bigger fish. You get the idea. *In reality, it's never been easier to get noticed by the right people without wasting a lot of money.* You just need to uncover the Big Idea that will captivate the senses of the critical few—give them an experience so rare that they will want to spread the message to everyone they know as a way to elevate their own status within the group.

What we can learn from this shift is that forcing people doesn't work. Trying to muscle your way into their minds by buying more media to recite a mediocre message will backfire. Most ads try to do this. In many cases, advertising is nothing more than an acceptable form of propaganda. In his book on mass movements, *The True Believer*, Eric Hoffer wrote:

> The truth seems to be that propaganda on its own cannot force its way into unwilling minds; neither can it inculcate something wholly new; nor can it keep people persuaded once they have ceased to believe. It penetrates only into minds already open, and rather than instill opinion it articulates and justifies opinions already present in the minds of its recipients. The gifted propagandist brings to a boil ideas and passions already simmering in the minds of his hearers. He echoes their innermost feelings. Where opinion is not coerced, people can be made to believe only in what they already "know."[9]

For this reason, the visibility of online webpages developed by users are out-competing companies' own sites. Intelliseek CMO and CEO Pete Blackshaw and Mike Nazzaro, wrote, "The same high-rated links that marketers work so hard to achieve often share the same real estate as heavily-trafficked consumer-generated links and personal websites, yet the CGM [consumer generated media] links often carry far higher credibility and trust."[10]  In fact, according to Intelliseek research, more than 60 percent of consumers trust other consumers' online postings.[11]

People trust people. People trust their own group to help define what they'd like more than they trust marketers. Sell to social animals rather than customer profiles.

# PART III

## An Anthropological, Historical, and Psychological Analysis of **TALK**

*This section represents the research "meat" on why we talk. If you want a deeper understanding of why your customers communicate, this treatise will be both engaging and enlightening. We'll discuss various areas of research and psychological disciplines to help deepen your understanding of human communication and how it relates to your business.*

# LANGUAGE:
## THE ANATOMY OF COMMUNICATION

> For millions of years, mankind lived just like the animals. Then something happened which unleashed the power of our imagination. We learned to talk, we learned to listen. Speech has allowed the communication of ideas enabling people to work together … to build the impossible.[1]
>
> —Stephen Hawking

My mother says I started talking when I was seven months old. I said, "Agua," which is Spanish for water, and I haven't stopped talking since. I love the brain buzz of a good conversation. Nothing in the world thrills me more than the drama of life: Learning something new, finding out about a great new gadget, or the next new thing.

At only seven months, I discovered the ability to formulate my own communication by mimicking the world around me. Amazing! I translated the sounds I heard into vibrations with my vocal cords and conveyed something meaningful to my parents. I discovered the power of communication. Understanding what I have done naturally now for twenty-six years, however, has not been as simple and natural as the conversion that happened in my brain as baby. We often hear that you have to crawl before you can walk. You also must listen before you can speak.

How word-of-mouth really works is understood when one contemplates this miracle of infancy. Now the question has become, as my mother constantly asked, "¿Por qué hablas tanto?"—"Why do you talk so much?"

## The New Tower of Babel

> The Lord said, "If as one people speaking the same language they have begun to do this, then nothing they plan to do will be impossible for them. Come, let us go down and confuse their language so they will not understand each other." (Genesis 11: 6-7)

Speaking stirs the imagination. The World Wide Web helps information reconnect to itself at lightening speed. The modern-day Tower of Babel is the Internet, where Chinese children can communicate in real time with American kids using online translators. This new Tower is overcoming the language barrier and unifying cultures of people through a single interactive environment where we all "talk."

The implications of the Internet have industries wishing they could play the role of LORD and knock the tower down. But why? After all, by leaving the Tower standing, marketers can capitalize on biologically-rooted traits, a superior and more effective strategy for marketing, to sell their products rather than using propaganda and repetition—a far less effective strategy—to convince consumers to buy their products.

When man developed language, he began advancing at a rapid rate. Knowledge became easily transmittable across generations: Father to son, mother to daughter. It is through talking that people are able to communicate and express their ideas and beliefs efficiently. Talking has helped us build the impossible—from the pyramids of Egypt to the transatlantic cable.

## Satisfying a Basic Need

This need to communicate is just as evident in lower primates as it is in humans. In the 1960s, psychologists R. Allen Gardner and

Beatrice Gardner carried out a study with a chimpanzee named Washoe, to whom they wanted to teach American Sign Language (ASL). Previous studies had shown that chimpanzees' vocal apparatus is not well-suited for speaking. Gardner and Gardner concluded that "sign language is an appropriate medium of two-way communication for the chimpanzee."[2]

Whether or not chimpanzees can acquire a structured language is unimportant. What is important to understand, however, is that the chimpanzees had a desire to communicate for their own benefit. Concerning these studies, the director of the Center for Cognitive Neuroscience at MIT, Stephen Pinker, concludes, "The features of the symbol system were deliberately designed by scientists and acquired by the chimps because it was useful for them then and there."[3] By communicating in a way that made the experimenters happy, the chimps were rewarded. They benefited from communicating through hand signals.

Consider another study conducted by Leavens and Hopkins. Chimpanzees were placed in an environment with an experimenter and an out-of-reach food source that was accessible to the experimenter. While observing the chimpanzees' behavior, they noted that out of 115 of them, 53 pointed at the food; all of them tried to indicate to the experimenter that they wanted the experimenter to pass the food to them by pointing or using alternating glances. This isn't particularly impressive except that in the wild, chimpanzees are not known to exhibit pointing behavior, and only three of the chimpanzees in the experiment had been trained to do so.[4] *The chimpanzees developed a communicative gesture in order to satisfy their needs. Humans developed communication to satisfy their needs too.*

Communication for one's benefit is universal. It is not limited to only chimpanzees and humans; rather, it is prevalent across the animal kingdom, from ants to birds. *Communication in order to achieve a benefit is inescapable. This is the crux of word-of-mouth.*

Like chimpanzees, small children, unaware of the names of objects, often point to what they want. As they learn an object's name, the frequency of pointing decreases. By adulthood, pointing accounts for only 5% of all gestures.[5] As children grow, the rather crude communication—pointing—gets replaced by language.

Like gestures, language has arisen in communities where it benefits the individuals' interests. For example, on many slave plantations, people from different backgrounds were required to work together. Cooperation was difficult because they did not speak the same language. Over time, however, a language arose based upon the language of the plantation owners. These languages weren't grammatically correct; rather, words from the original language were strung together without regard to syntax.[6] The development of these languages, technically termed Pidgins, enabled the slaves to communicate and carry out their lives more efficiently.

Even though these people did not know the "new" language of the plantation owners, they selected words and assigned meanings in order to make communication easier. What is even more amazing is what happened when the children of these Pidgin speakers started to develop language: It achieved a grammatical structure. In other words, the second-generation language, called Creole, took on an organized syntax. Creole is not the product of imitation, as it neither resembles the parents' usage nor does it accurately reflect the original language from which the Creole was derived. The children created a grammatical structure where none existed previously. They now had a full language ready for use. And interestingly, this phenomenon is not limited to those who speak with their mouths. It has been extensively studied in a deaf community in Nicaragua.[7]

## The Language Instinct

An explanation for this phenomenon is that young children possess an instinct to acquire language in a sensible structure. Stephen Pinker, who aptly termed this the "language instinct," writes:

Language … is not a cultural artifact that we learn the way we tell time or how the federal government works. Instead, it is a distinct piece of the biological makeup of our brains. Language is a complex, specialized skill, which develops in the child spontaneously, without conscious effort or formal instruction, is developed without awareness of its underlying logic, is qualitatively the same in every individual, and is distinct from more general abilities to process information or behave intelligently.[8]

Language, therefore, is possibly just as biologically-rooted as is the sensation of pain. Both pain sensation and language confer biological advantages: Pain allows us to recognize that we are being harmed, and *language allows us to communicate our needs and wants.*

This "language instinct" is reflected in the capacity of language acquisition. Estimates on the number of words that the average American high-school graduate can understand are in the range of 60,000[9] to 80,000[10] — astounding when you consider Shakespeare used only 15,000 words in his writings.[11]

These numbers do not account for the quantity of words people actively use, but rather the number they can understand. For example, if I presented you with a made-up word like "confuddled," although you hadn't heard it before, you could instantly decipher it to be a composite of the words *confused* and *befuddled.*

This ability to understand a vast amount of words without previously encountering some of them is a testament to efficacy of language in communication. We are able to understand what people are saying (understand their communication) even though we may not be familiar with every word they are using.

The ability of a three-year-old child to use language is no less amazing than the high school graduate. Although a three-year-old child is virtually incapable of completing most adult tasks, he can obey language "rules far more often than flouting them, respecting language universals, erring in sensible, adult-like ways, and avoiding many kinds of errors altogether."[12]

## Reciprocal Altruism

In considering the origins of language in early hunter-gatherer societies, language, at first glance, appears to be a liability due to the alerting nature of the voice; for instance, talking could startle an animal you are trying to kill for dinner.[13] How then, is language regarded as an advantage? In asking this question, Michael C. Corballis, psychology professor at the University of Auckland, gives three answers: One, language is arbitrary, allowing it to distinguish between objects that iconic representation may confuse (hand positions mimicking the shape of the object). Two, it allows people to communicate in the dark. Three, it allows the hands and mouth to be used simultaneously for different purposes, such as explaining and demonstrating the use of a tool.[14] All three of these reasons illustrate the efficacy of language.

Based upon an individual's biological motivations to propagate his or her genes, it appears that these communicative tools would be directed towards revealing a new food source to kin, while keeping it a secret from other members of the group.

What happens in many groups of animals, however, is the opposite. The one that discovers an advantage, such as the food source, will inform other members of the group about it. At first glance, this seems to destroy that animal's new-found advantage, but it supports *reciprocal altruism*: If you scratch my back, I'll scratch yours. The food source will inevitably run out. The animal will then need another food source, likely to be discovered by another animal in the group. By sharing the information, it is more likely to ensure the survival of the group as a whole.

In addition to the survival advantage gained by sharing information, in primates a social advantage is also conferred to the individual sharing information. By providing information beneficial to the group, one achieves a higher social status as a valuable group resource. In the long run, the animal benefits by sharing, giving his lineage a greater chance for survival.

We can relate. When we tell others something good, we benefit. For this reason, we love to scratch each other's backs. This back-scratching reveals our need to be part of a social group to protect us against adversity and nature. In order to ensure group stability, these groups develop dialects and jargon that allow them to mark others as insiders or outsiders. These dialects constantly change to reveal people who are looking to benefit from the group without supporting it.[15]

Language, as British anthropologist Robin Dunbar writes, permits "us to exchange information relevant to our ability to survive in a complex, constantly changing social world, but it also allows us to mark other individuals as friend or foe."[16]

## A Love Affair with Research

Marketing's love affair with research has created a language all its own, and it's a language the consumer doesn't speak. Yet how many times have we seen television commercials where scripts are taken verbatim from a research summary? This is the limitation of research: It doesn't translate literally into the consumer-driven marketplace. Communicating and connecting with our feelings is a challenge on its own, and the problem is exacerbated when marketing teams fail to translate research jargon into communication that connects with their audience. For an example, go to: http://www.whywetalk.com/beerguys.

Communication and language are intricately-connected and bio-logically-rooted. People communicate to "control their environment so as to acquire needed resources."[17] Language is the most efficient means of communication available, and has facilitated the worldwide dominance of *Homo sapiens*.

## The Illusion of WOM Marketing

So what does this mean? People talk without our help. Today, marketing companies promise to generate word-of-mouth, but the idea of hiring word-of-mouth doesn't work. Hiring word-of-mouth opposes our nature, which is inclined to share information that makes us important to our group rather than setting us up to be liars. The idea of hiring "pretend fans" often backfires.

If you've ever read a book about "buzz" or "word-of-mouth marketing" and tried applying what you learned, you invariably discovered you were unable to ignite a peer-to-peer frenzy. These authors, although well-intentioned, didn't understand the mechanisms behind why we talk. As a consequence, these step-by-step WOM-producing strategies will likely fail.

No one knows the magic formula that forces people to jump around and tell the world about your new product. *People talk to serve their needs. If telling someone about a new product does not benefit them, they won't talk.*

Knowing this made writing this book a challenge. In truth, there is not much to say about word-of-mouth. Essentially, "word-of-mouth" is the label we use to refer to a phenomenon we don't understand; this ignorance gave rise to the idea of "word-of-mouth-marketing"—and the idea is crazy because it can't be created by marketers.

It's important to realize that there are certain biological and psychological realities that make people talk. *If you give someone something to talk about, they will.* Once they start talking, let 'em go. Don't try to manipulate the conversation—sit back, listen and learn how to create the next thing that will amuse and surprise your customers, giving them a reason to keep talking.

After *The Power of Cult Branding* was released, people asked: "How do you create a cult brand?" The answer is, you don't. Consumers do. *All you can do is become something worth talking about.* Becoming a cult brand is not about knowing demographics and psychographics—those are not the determinants. If you want to spawn brand evangelists, you will do well to understand the concepts of influencers (See *The Principle of* Influence in Part III), trust (see *The Principle of Trust* in Part III), habit, and experience.

## WOM Subsets: Gossip and Rumor

Business currently recognizes the *effect* of "Word-of-Mouth Marketing" rather than the *cause* behind why people talk. It is perhaps unfortunate that marketers have globally labeled customer-driven information transmissions as "word-of-mouth," as there are important subsets to consider like gossip and rumor.

In a study on rumor, marketing professors Michael Kamins and Valerie Folkes from the University of Southern California, and Lars Perner from San Diego State University revealed that "WOM differs from rumor in that it is the conduit through which rumor is spread."[18] This is comparable to the pipes carrying liquids through your house. All the pipes (the *conduits*) channel a liquid from one place to another. The liquids (like water or sewage) they channel vary. It would be confusing to group the fluids and the pipes together under the category of "pipes"—the fluid they are a conduit for is significant! And this is essentially what happens when we labeled all talk as "word-of-mouth."

Some marketers separate rumor from word-of-mouth, but still consider them comparable entities. While not the ideal distinction, it is an important one to make. Rumors often start without any basis in fact (for example, the energy drink Red Bull was rumored to contain bull sperm). Rumors are hard, if not impossible, to predict, as they often have no relevance to the product itself. As a result, they can only be dealt with as they arise. Many companies, like Red Bull, actively monitor and quell rumors through public relations efforts like publishing FAQs on their websites. After all, you wouldn't want people to think you were selling sperm juice!

Luckily for your businesses, it has been shown that "once the WOM information is labeled as rumor, it is perceived as less credible. Respondents spread 30 percent of the rumors they heard, but generally believe that an average of 26 percent of rumors are actually true."[19] People perceive most rumors to be false, and the rate of transmission indicates that people are likely to pass on only those rumors they believe are true, which they filter by the information's credibility and their own personal beliefs.

And with this in mind, did you hear about what Tom Cruise did …

# GOSSIP:
## THE BACKBONE OF WOM

An old Scandinavian fable pictures the world as struggling helplessly within the slimy coils of a gigantic sea-serpent called Midyard. The social world is within the grip of no fabulous sea-monster, but it is entangled and worried by a serpentine species comprising forms running all the way from the elusive wrigglers of private life to the hydra-headed monster that throws coil after coil about nations and organizations of nations. This species is a type of communication; it is gossip.[1]

—Frederick Elmore Lumley

*I do it, you do it, and my mother is the queen of it.*

What most marketers term "word-of-mouth" is really gossip's cousin. While gossip is about people, the gossip marketers try to create is about products. In order to understand product-gossip, it is necessary to understand the more traditional gossip—the people-gossip we all love most.

Gossip is everywhere. Social conversation takes up two-thirds of all human conversation[2] and gossip accounts for a significant chunk. As the Spanish saying goes, *I don't like gossip, but it really entertains me!* Humans enjoy talking, but our real addiction is gossiping. You can hear it all through the grapevine.

Gossiping is our favorite pasttime, and we are good at it! Tabloids and tabloid-like TV shows exist because we love gossip. We've been doing it for a very long time. Contrary to popular belief, gossip is not just idle chit-chat; rather, gossip serves to establish and maintain social ties.

In *Psychology Today*, Nigel Nicholson, professor of Organizational Behavior at London Business School, divides gossip's function in the social sphere into three categories: Networking, influencing, and alliances.[3] Each of these are inextricably linked. Via networking, people ascertain the relative position of others in the social hierarchy and seek to gain the favor of these high-ranking individuals. Influence is what people use to both gain rank and form ties with those in high-ranking positions. The benefit people provide to the group is directly correlated to their position. As Nicholson writes, "When we find an opportunity, we try to advance a good opinion about ourselves to those who can help us."[4]

Both networking and influence are products of the third category: Alliances. The prerequisite for networking and influence is people to associate with. Without a group, there's no status ranking.

Gossip satisfies this "basic need to acquire information about the personal and intimate aspects of other people's lives."[5] When people gossip, they are providing what is perceived as exclusive "insider information." Exclusivity often proves useful to the group, especially if the information gives the members an advantage because it's about people they know, as is often the case. Perhaps more than anything, people are interested in other people, especially those like themselves. The usefulness of this information is credited to the bearer of the information, marking him or her as valuable to the group, resulting in the conferring of status and prestige.

## Enforcing the Moral Code

Gossip also solidifies a group's value systems. Robin Westen writes, "Gossip serves important social and psychological functions; it's the unifying force that communicates a group's moral code. It's the social glue that holds us all together."[6] Gossip perpetuates the "moral code" by relaying stories that reveal social transgressions. In transmitting the message, the transmitter is judging a person's behavior as outside of the group's "code." The judgment is reinforced by the group's reaction to the news, which ultimately reinforces the strength of the group. Former professor of philosophy Robert Goodman observes:

> Analysis shows that gossip promotes friendship and group cohesion, helps to sustain group norms, and often serves to effectively communicate important information. Social scientists also emphasize that gossip may be important to the extent that it provides a basis for the comparison of an individual's experiences, feelings, and beliefs with those of others; contributes to one's sense of self esteem by revealing other people's failings; and enhances status among peers.[7]

Reinforcing group ties is perhaps the reason negative gossip is more prevalent than positive gossip. In his seminal work *The Presentation of Self In Everyday Life*, Erving Goffman explains that "secret derogation seems to be much more common than secret praise, perhaps because such derogation seems to maintain the solidarity of the team, demonstrating mutual regard at the expense of those absent."[8]

Imagine a group of four people: Ben, Matt, Alan, and Harvey. Ben, Matt, and Alan are having lunch. Alan brings up a piece of news about Harvey. If this news is positive information, it either maintains the four-person group (if the news does not violate the "moral code") or it solidifies the four-person group (if it depicts Harvey adhering to the "code" in an exemplary fashion). If, however, the gossip depicts a transgression by Harvey, it reinforces the bond between Ben, Matt, and Alan, a three-person group, and distances Harvey slightly.

Now imagine these four people as four balls. It's much harder to fit four balls into a tight space than three. Three objects can be more closely associated than four. The negative gossip, therefore, results in a stronger association amongst the three than the positive gossip would. Relating to this desire to form closely-knit groups, groups, Aaron Ben-Ze'ev, professor of philosophy at the University of Haifa, writes:

Gossip also satisfies the tribal need, namely, the need to belong and be accepted by a unique group. One meaning of 'gossip' is indeed 'being a friend of.' The sharing of intimate and personal information and the intimate manner of conveying this information contribute to the formation of an exclusive group with intimate and affectionate ties between its members.[9]

As Ben-Ze'ev hints, the meaning of gossip is closely linked with the idea of a tight group. The word gossip derives from the Anglo-Saxon word *godsibb*, meaning a godparent or a "spiritual relative." Eventually, it came to mean a close friend. Later, it took on the meaning of a person who engages in idle talk, probably because close friends participate in such activities.[10]

## Gossip and Grooming

Remember the last time you went to the zoo and saw a group of chimpanzees grooming each other? The playing and picking each other's fur serves a social purpose that unifies the group, much in the same way gossip does. By establishing these groups, the chimpanzees gain protection from other groups. There is safety in numbers. A social hierarchy also exists, with higher positions occupied by those who can provide the most benefit, including things like strength and information.

The most popular studies on gossip, grooming, and groups were conducted by Robin Dunbar. Dunbar asserted that "language evolved to allow us gossip,"[11] and that "language evolved as a 'cheap' form of social grooming, thereby enabling the ancestral humans to maintain the cohesion of the unusually large groups demanded by the particular conditions they faced at the time."[12] Even though gossip did not likely evolve directly from grooming, both gossip and grooming form social ties and social groups.

A consensus emerged from these studies: Gossip and grooming serve analogous functions. Even Dunbar's critics agree. One of these critics, the psychologist Michael C. Corballis, provided a more generally accepted interpretation of the evidence: "My guess is that Dunbar's argument might be more plausible if inverted; the selective pressures for the evolution of language probably had to do with propositional communication, and this secondarily solved the problem of social grooming among large groups."[13] *Language evolved as a means of communication, and, as a byproduct, was a great facilitator for social grooming.*

## The Need for Groups

The need to form groups goes back deep into our history. You can see the power of this need expressed in the most widespread religion on the planet: Christianity. In his work on the history of Christianity, Kenneth Scott Latourette outlined a litany of factors affecting Christianity's success. Prominent among these was its ability to generate an incredibly close-knit group. Latourette writes, "Not one of its rivals possessed so powerful and coherent a structure as did the Church. No other gave its adherents quite the same feeling of coming into a closely knit community."[14]

The status and protection afforded by groups is an inescapable human need, with the measure of status in these groups being the amount of information the individual provides. Robin Westen succinctly sums up the importance of an individual to a group:

> Gossip ... defines who's in and who's out in a group. If you're considered worthy enough to be buzzed about on the grapevine, you're in. If you've got 'valuable' information to show, you're also in. But if you don't fit into either group, consider yourself out of the loop, and out to lunch—alone.[15]

Social psychologist Ralph Rosnow's studies have revealed that those who hold the highest status in a group are those who maintain the balance of being both a gossipee and a gossiper; in other words, those who provide information and are worthy of being talked about themselves rule the kingdom.[16] Gossiping about someone, while strengthening the social ties of those present, also humanizes the person transgressing.[17] Everyone realizes that he or she will most likely transgress eventually, and observing other people's transgressions is endearing. When this same person gossips, he or she is supplying valued information to the group and it reinforces social ties. The person maintaining the gossiper/gossipee balance, then, becomes someone very much like yourself who also provides a lot of information—an individual you are likely to value.

## Product-Based Groups

Gossip about people is undeniably essential to the establishment and maintenance of groups and group dynamics. How then does group gossip relate to hypersonic product-gossip? In his book on an early Internet community, Howard Rheingold made the astute observation that "people who come up with accurate and well-worded answers win prestige, in front of the whole virtual stadium."[18] The Internet provides the perfect medium for product discussion. You can communicate with someone you've never met, and possibly will never meet, on the other side of the screen. You can send someone a message faster than you can go knock on your neighbor's door. Most importantly, you can broadcast your message to thousands just as quickly.

The Internet has spawned virtual communities around common interests. These interests range from the general to the extremely specific—from magic tricks to obscure, difficult sleight-of-hand maneuvers with a deck of cards. Some group, somewhere, is likely discussing whatever you can imagine.

Rheingold observed that within these groups, those who are most useful gain the highest status. The currency of status is *information*. Many of these groups are organized around product discussions, and the commodity is product-gossip. Instead of people, products are relevant as this is the basis for the group. People won't hesitate to let others know which product is great and which one sucks.

Unlike traditional gossip, there is no need to worry about product-gossip getting back to the source, as inanimate objects don't care. Telling other people about a product's faults, if the information is correct, is no less valuable than providing positive feedback. While the negative information is awful for the product developer, it is great for the product-gossiper as its relevancy will prove helpful to the group and confer status.

The strengths of these groups can be incredible: People treat those they encounter in the community as friends and are willing to lend support when needed.

From a marketer's perspective, this is important because people are more likely to believe information coming from friends with expertise than almost any other source. These people have an extremely strong influence, and it's strengthening with more groups, more voices, and more efficient mediums for exchange.

While this spells doom for poor products, it is great news for those offering a great product or service, and it is possible to maximize product-gossip. Before we consider the necessary conditions for product-gossip, let's look at how product-gossip groups are connected.

# CONNECTEDNESS:
## THE ARCHITECTURE OF GOSSIP

> No man is an island, entire of itself; every man is a
> piece of the continent, a part of the main.
>
> –John Donne, *Meditation XVII*

We are connected and we depend upon each other to survive physically and psychologically. People make our lives better or worse by how they relate to us. It's been said that people are our connection to the rest of the world, but how connected are we? How many degrees of separation are really between you and Kevin Bacon?

## Six Degrees of Separation

The landmark study on connectedness was memorialized in the late Yale University psychologist Stanley Milgram's paper "The Small World Problem." It sought to answer the question: *Just how connected are we?*

Participants were to mail the package to someone they knew who was likely to get it closer to the target. In one study, the target was a stockbroker from Sharon, Massachusetts. The letters originated from three locations: A random person in Nebraska, a person in Nebraska who was a stockbroker, and a random person in Boston. Twenty-nine percent of the packages reached the target, with a higher percentage of people in the Nebraska stockbroker and Boston random categories reaching the target.[1]

Milgram concluded that, on average, people were separated from anyone else in the world by six degrees. In other words, the message would have to be passed along an average of five times before reaching the target.[2]

A second conclusion—one more pertinent to product marketers—is that not only can information get trapped incredibly easily, but it is, in fact, likely to get trapped. This likelihood is reflected in the 29 percent success rate that Milgram observed. Even if someone is looking for a way to pass information to a target, the person may be ill-equipped to do so. It is possible a message could be passed on in two steps, but that person may never see that connection. Although you may be incredibly close to the person you are trying to reach, you may not be able to see it.[3]

The problem with this study, from a product standpoint, is it reveals more about decision-making than social interaction. Information does not get passed along by consumers the way it did in Milgram's experiments. Even if you had a team of consumers willing to preach to the masses, it doesn't mean they have a clue which channels to distribute information about your product into for product-gossip to take off.

## The Strength of Weak Ties: A Lumpy Bowl of Oatmeal

People don't intentionally plan for communication to reach a target they've never met nor heard about. Given the number of products that fail, we would guess (given real conditions) that the success rate is much lower than Milgram's observed twenty-nine percent. The more people you get talking, however, the more likely the information is to pass between channels. From this, we can infer that there must be multiple groups talking simultaneously in order to ensure our product-gossip takes flight. To understand this problem, we have to wonder, *how does information get passed between groups?*

The answer was discovered by Stanford professor and sociological theorist Mark Granovetter and published in his paper "The Strength of Weak Ties." Granovetter concluded that it is casual acquaintances (weak ties) that can put you and your information in contact with a diverse range of groups. In Granovetter's words: "Weak ties are more likely to link members of *different* small groups than are strong ones, which tend to favor local cohesion, but overall fragmentation."[4]

If you think about it, Granovetter's conclusion makes sense. The individuals you know well are likely to know others in your circle, or at least people similar to those in your circle. Information disseminated to these close friends (strong ties) is likely to circle in a small environment and get trapped. When giving information to a casual acquaintance, however, the acquaintance is likely to have strong ties with people in circles different than yours. Those groups best positioned to distribute information, therefore, are those composed of many casual acquaintances (i.e., many weak ties).[5]

Milgram and Granovetter's work has been expanded significantly in recent years. In one 2002 study, for the first time in nearly four decades, Milgram's 1967 study was challenged. University of Alaska psychologist Judith Kleinfeld published a paper taking a fresh look at Milgram's study, reviewing the original papers and the data locked away in archives. Kleinfeld focused on how selecting participants who had links via location or occupation created a bias toward figures on connectivity. She concluded that "rather than living in a 'small, small world,' we may live in a world that looks a lot like a bowl of lumpy oatmeal, with many small worlds loosely connected and perhaps some small worlds not connected at all."[6]

Kleinfeld's analysis is similar to a comment made by Milgram in his initial paper: Certain people were noticeably more active in passing the message to the final target (i.e., there are few ways to pass information from one group to another).[7] Just as Kleinfeld suggests, the small worlds are loosely connected by a few channels.

## The Science of Networks

In recent years, a new science termed "the science of networks" involving the collaboration of people from multiple disciplines, such as physics, sociology, and mathematics, has emerged. In his book *Six*

*Degrees: The Science of A Connected Age*, Duncan J. Watts, a pioneer in this field, recounts the developments in this new science that seeks to find mathematically-based models for social interaction. The accuracy with which these models can predict interacting events is startling. These scientists discovered that if social networks were viewed as a picture, "most nodes (people) will be relatively poorly connected, while a select minority will be very highly connected."[8] Just as Milgram and Kleinfeld observed, people with more connections are better equipped to pass along a message than others.

Those highly connected tend to attract more connections than those poorly connected. This is the same phenomenon driving the networking and the formation of alliances through gossip. Those with a higher position (the most connections) are likely to be the most attractive individuals to associate with due to the benefits they confer. This phenomenon is what sociologist Robert Merton coined "The Matthew Effect."[9] As Watts writes, "Social identity ... drives the creation of social networks."[10]

## The Online World Strengthens Weak Ties

The structure of the Internet has important implications for information diffusion along social channels. Put simply, *the Internet strengthens weak ties.*

Almost any product or topic you can think of is discussed on the Internet. When you post on message boards or review sites, you are connecting with people you've never met. If your information is perceived as valuable, you achieve status. Amazon.com has learned to identify and reward these coveted product reviewers by providing reviewer rankings with "Top Reviewer" status.

Social status and group membership is clearly reflected in online discussion groups. Many people engaging in these discussions participate daily. Certain names become familiar, and based on the quality of information these people have provided in the past, you may evaluate the validity of their statements.

While most relationships forged in person are the result of proximity or occupation, in the online world, people organize themselves by interests, atypical of real-world interaction. In person, you aren't likely to regularly talk to people who have a shared interest in Red Bull, and it is unlikely that you will gain social status as a result of your Red Bull knowledge. In the online world, the opposite is true.

The online world offers a unique merger between the strength of weak ties and the strength of friendship in the dissemination of product-gossip. Due to discussions centering around certain topics and products, you are likely to encounter people you would not otherwise encounter in normal daily activity. For example, a corporate lawyer may find and trust information about a book supplied by a gardener on another continent, a very unlikely partnership. The lawyer may pass the information to other lawyer friends on the same continent. The information, then, has easily traveled between diverse circles in a way that would be almost impossible without the Internet.

Oftentimes, individuals in an online discussion group share information about products or topics that have nothing to do with the main focus of the community. Some groups even have sections for unrelated topics. An individual may find something particularly valuable and think others will want to know. People are likely to listen, especially if they have found that person's comments valuable.

## Forging Friendships Online

For those who participate in online discussions regularly, an interesting phenomenon develops: The formation of friendships between people who have never met in person. Among these individuals, value or rank is determined by the validity of information and the connection forged with others as a result of past participation. The majority of people trust the recommendations of friends more than any other influence, in many cases even more than their past experience.[11] Discussion groups are a perfect mechanism for the formation and maintenance of friendships.

In one study, psychologists Carol Werner and Pat Parmelee at the University of Utah discovered friendships are not developed the way most people think. Most people tend to think they are drawn to people who have similar opinions and not because they participate in similar activities.[12] Conversely, Werner and Parmelee's "results suggest that the opportunity to engage in mutually pleasurable activities may be a stronger motive in friendship choice and friendship maintenance than is the satisfaction of knowing a friend agrees with you."[13] This reinforces the idea that regular participation in online discussion groups forges friendship, as you're discussing a subject both you and the other person are interested in, doing something you both enjoy (posting to the community boards).

Weak ties in the offline world become strong ties in the online world. And unlike strong offline ties, these strong ties are to people from diverse backgrounds, proving to be both highly and widely valuable to marketers. The Internet provides a platform for influencing the opinions of passersby (weak ties that will remain weak) and for developing very strong platforms of influence (by providing channels that allow strong ties to serve as bridges between groups), a very powerful mechanism for information diffusion.

## An Equality of Influence

There's another interesting dynamic to online discussion that does not manifest in face-to-face interaction. A study conducted by business professors Vitaly Dubrovsky from Clarkson University and Beheruz Sethna from University of West Georgia, and computer science professor Sara Kiesler from Carnegie Mellon University found:

> When the groups made decisions in face-to-face meetings, the high-status member dominated

discussions with the three low-status members. Also, the high-status member more often was a "first advocate" in the face-to-face discussions, and first advocates were more influential than later advocates. These status inequalities in face-to-face decision making were pronounced just when the high-status member's expertise was relevant to the decision task. When the same groups made comparable decisions using electronic mail, status and expertise inequalities in participation were reduced. A striking and unexpected result was that "first" advocacy was shared by high- and low-status members in discussions using electronic mail. This behavior resulted in increased equality of influence across status and expertise.[14]

The online world appears to level the playing field between groups of people with varying levels of influence. This doesn't mean status conferred by the presentation of helpful information doesn't hold weight; rather, people are more likely to say what they think about a product, and are quicker to do so. Without people present, posters are less likely to worry about being evaluated, and the nature of the medium may remove the normal considerations people would have when they are interacting with others.[15] Under normal circumstances, static cues like appearance and dynamic cues like behavior aid in the establishment of social positions. In the online environment, these cues are significantly weakened or absent.

People are likely to say whatever they think about a product in an online environment—good or bad. Acceptance of their opinions will confer status and membership in the group.

The genius mathematician Blaise Pascal said it best in 1685:

> Man is related to everything that he knows. And everything is both cause and effect, working and worked upon, mediate and immediate, all things

      mutually dependent. A bond that is both natural and
      imperceptible binds together things the most distant
      and things the most different.

A lumpy bowl of oatmeal connects the distant and strange together. Within weak-tie relationships lies the doorway to flourishing product-gossip—the keys to the Door of Talk are held by those we think are least likely to affect our success. At its core, this insight of weak ties challenges our current belief in demographics, psychographics, and all the familiar tools of marketing. We also gain new tools and insights that allow us to better understand the medium of consumer information transmission.

# SOCIAL SYSTEMS:
## WHERE WE TALK

*This chapter on social systems proved to be the most challenging. Although social systems and systems theory is not for the fainthearted, we simply couldn't complete a treatise on the nature of Talk without discussing group behavior and the role of the individual in the group. From the marketer's perspective, this valuable insight proves to be essential in understanding why your customers talk.*

A person goes to a party. Everyone brings Corona beer. The party is fun. The people are fun. Eventually, the person starts drinking Corona at home because the experiences associated with that beer are pleasurable. The person was taught that the group's preference was Corona. The experience confirmed it was a good choice. Being part of the group helps solidify the person's preference and confirms his or her sense of personal identity.

Behold the power of the social system: Group dynamics—not brand dynamics—shape individual preference.* So what fuels the social system? The answer is "individuals." Individuals behave for their own benefit, infusing the system with an over-riding sense of personal identity. Driven by this self-fulfilling need, the individual's influence fuels the actions of the group.

Social systems allow us to observe how humans behave inside familiar frameworks like work, family, chat rooms, organizations, or brand communities. *Social systems help us identify patterns that are of interest to the brands we manage.* Once we've identified the group by its behavior, we can look inside to understand the motivation of the individual.

---

* It should be noted, however, that even though social systems have greater impact on a person's behavior, the marketing for Corona reflects the need for fulfillment. Corona doesn't advertise the brand; they advertise the sweetness of the experience. But even the best marketing and advertising fights against the inertia of social pressure.

# A Group's Nucleus is the Individual

There are two accurate statements to be made about the individual and groups:

1- The individuals belonging to a social group *define* the group.
2- The individuals belonging to a social group are *defined* by the group.

Herein lies the complexity of social systems. If you only accept one of the above statements, you will most likely miss the pattern of what's creating consumer movement.

As in the old chicken and egg debate, which came first: The social group's influence on the individual or the individual's influence on the group social? Or from the marketers' perspectives, which do you study first? Convention says focus on the group (as in focus groups). But wisdom says *listen to the individual.*

Individuals don't necessarily see themselves as a part of any system, because from their point of view, communication is driven by their individual needs and what benefits them. *The social system supports their drives to feed their personal needs.* Very few groups are altruistic. The collective social group develops the pressures the individual consumers experience and then imposes them on themselves. The consumer conforms to that group, oddly enough, as a way to express his or her individuality.

Similarly to how a single cell holds the DNA of an entire human being, if you study any individual, you will see his or her imprint on the social system. Social groups don't shape people as much as people shape social groups. Social groups fulfill an individual's needs. *People find groups that hold the promise of fulfilling their sense of identity. The individual experience they take away from the group is what branding is all about.*

Marketers have a tendency to confuse the patterns of a system with definitive predictability, as is illustrated by the use of focus groups. Too many marketers use focus groups to analyze past behavior to predict future performance. The flaw in this thinking is that systems don't prevent new events from happening. As they say in the marketing of financial services, "Past performance is no guarantee of future results."

## Probability Blindness

The challenge of speaking about humans as a social system, group, or collective mind is that you are trying to hit a moving target.

For example, imagine you want to predict a coin flip. Is the next flip going to be heads or tails? If you start recording each flip, patterns will emerge. Heads. Tails. Heads. Heads. Heads. Tails. Heads. Tails. And on and on. Realize, each flip is independent of the previous flip—the past and the future are not connected. The odds are fifty-fifty: Heads or tails. There's nothing mysterious about this, but here is where the math gets interesting. Any pattern you see is a mathematical illusion or a recording of the past.

Heads. Tails. Tails. Tails. Tails. Tails. Tails. What is more likely to show up next, heads or tails? The accumulation of tails at this point makes it feel like the next flip will be heads or tails, depending upon how you perceive the pattern. Of course, in reality, the same mathematical probability of heads or tails emerges with each toss: Still fifty-fifty.

This "probability blindness" makes predictive models like demographics flawed in assessing human behavior. Most demographic research is a snapshot of the past. Like the next coin toss, however, the next consumer direction is independent of the past actions.

Each consumer is a person, with his or her own world of ideas, concepts, opinions, and dreams—all surrounding a sense of personal identity. What we've learned so far from this treatise on Talk is that *communication happens to benefit the individual.* Nothing affects a person's decision to talk more than the trust of a friend. They want to share information they perceive as useful and that does not make them vulnerable to having a perspective in conflict with the opinions of the person or the group.

## The Collective Mind

If you can make your brand the hallmark for the desires of a group, the collective force of the group will imprint itself on the individual; when someone buys a Harley-Davidson motorcycle and starts attending rallies, they will start identifying with the attitudes of the group at the rallies and will, without conscious control, start to integrate that attitude into their lifestyle, at least when riding the motorcycle. When brands become linked with lifestyles, it's very unlikely customers will deflect, as doing so would mean denying a part of their personalities.

Systems theory helps us understand both the individual parts and the holistic nature of the life of our customers. If we focus on the group without putting the individual under the microscope, we miss the richness of their life and how brand experiences manifest for them. Yet if we only focus on the individual, we miss the broad strokes of the larger customer patterns.

The concept of the Collective Mind of the customer is crucial to understanding the best and highest use of word-of-mouth. Let's look at the Collective Mind principle in animal behavior to get a clearer picture.

Researcher Wayne Potts studied the aerial maneuvers of large flocks of Dunlin birds to see if there was a correlation between the group mentality and behavior. It was postulated that a single bird or small group of birds was signaling movements to the rest of the flock or that they were adjusting to the movements of their neighbors, but Potts found the time it would take individual birds to respond to the signals was four to five time slower than the rate of the flock's movements.[1]

The flock moved at a faster rate than the sum of the rates that would be calculated from the individual members.

The collective customer behaves in the same manner: As the group shifts, the speed of change increases with respect to the group rather than the individual members. In the 1940s, it was thought that running a four-minute mile was impossible. In 1954, Roger Bannister broke the four-minute barrier—an amazing feat. Within a month and a half, the four-minute barrier was broken again. It is now a standard for top athletes. Once the barrier in the running community was broken, the new standard spread quickly, enabling a large number of individuals to surpass a mark that was once thought to be impossible.

This collective group behavior can be either problematic or laden with potential. If you are caught manipulating word-of-mouth, the collective disapproval toward your brand can unfold at break-neck speed. However, it you truly embrace the behavior of the critical few that are important to your brand (and embracing may mean getting out of their way and letting them do their own thing), then you may very well see a swell of brand evangelism.

## The Competitive Advantage of Human Potential

Back in the 1960s, eminent psychologist Dr. Abraham Maslow predicted, "Human potential will be the primary source of competitive advantage in almost every industry."[2] He couldn't have been more right. Although he was offering this insight to managers about their workforce, he was essentially referring to how the seemingly subordinate employees hold the true power over those we normally cast in the dominant management role.

For decades, companies have acted as if the consumer was subordinate to their marketing powers. As we've seen, those days are gone. *The consumer has won.* Companies that think they are in control and behave as if they don't trust consumers to make up their own minds are eroding their own credibility. In trying to control the outcome by inserting themselves into consumers' conversations, the brand is doomed to mediocrity.

If we can take the liberty of paraphrasing Mr. Maslow, we would say, "Human potential will be the primary source of competitive advantage for almost every brand." Consumers have the potential to make your brand. If there's a potential for like-minded consumers to find each other and communicate, the possibility exists for the development of a faithful coalition around your brand. *Learn to respect the consumers' potential. Get out of their way and let them do their thing. They trust each other more than they trust you.*

Of course, this "freedom-for-the-customer" mentality flies in the face of some other well-known marketing thinkers. Sergio Zyman, former CMO of Coca-Cola, wrote, "The sole purpose of marketing is to sell more to more people, more often, and at higher prices."[3] Zyman also claimed that as marketers, "Customers are dangerous, and if you let them decide how they want to be satisfied, you're going to have a terrible time living up to their dreams."[4] Then again, he launched one of the biggest failures in brand history: New Coke. No one asked for it, and no one wanted it. When you think you are smarter than the consumer, you stop listening. Zyman said, "It's better if you can control both the promise and the delivery."[5] Maybe, but so what? *The important thing to recognize is you cannot control the consumer experience, which is the source of word-of-mouth.* When we say brands belong to the consumer, we mean a brand is defined by the consumer's experience with the brand.

When we go into the customer's world, it should be to do in-depth interviews, to understand their experiences, and to see how the fabric of common experiences is woven into their social system. With standard focus groups, consumers react to conceptual ideas in a rational manner because they cannot experience them. They cannot imagine the experience until they've partaken of it. The addiction to the high doesn't come from the drug; the addiction is to the experience one has as a result of taking, or taking the drug.

## Conscious Acceptance at the Group Level

The decision to congregate around a brand is not usually the result of individual choice, but rather of a group consciousness. There is a conscious acceptance of a brand at the group level. Fashion and fads are a good example of how quickly things heat up and cool down. The collective mind takes precedence over individual choice—and that's why it happens so quickly.

"Man is a perpetually wanting animal," Maslow noted, referring to man as a creature that is constantly trying to fulfill his needs. These needs, as we know, range from the physiological to the spiritual.

Maslow offered considerable insight into the nature of the individual. Maslow's *Hierarchy of Human Needs* illustrates that all human beings must fulfill their basic needs before progressing to higher concerns. Essentially, humans fulfill their needs at the bottom level of the pyramid and work their way up.[6]

**MASLOW'S HEIRARCHY** *of Human Needs*

Maslow's work reveals the underlying drivers of human behavior and decision-making. Although he never mentions the word "brand" in his books, his *Hierarchy of Human Needs* and concepts like *self-actualization* and *belongingness* are key to understanding why consumers consistently choose one brand over another and enjoy such a strong relationship with them.

## The Ultimate Goal of Branding: Self-Actualization

Why is fulfilling higher-level needs so integral to building strong relationships with customers? Higher-level needs influence future human behavior more than lower-level needs. Brands that fulfill higher-level needs become irreplaceable in the customer's mind.

To establish the very highest level of brand passion, the brand must offer a sense of self-actualization. In sports, this is done when the fan and the team (or hero) become one in the same. A hero is a person chosen by the "tribe" as an icon for its beliefs. The hero represents the hopes and dreams of the tribesmen, a voyeuristic fantasy beyond their current reality. As tribesmen watch the hero (or team's) journey, they project themselves into this immortal figure. The hero or team is a mirror of the fan's personal identity—and because of that, they are forever interconnected. If the fan can't see himself (at some level) as the hero or team—if he can't identify with the hero's plight—the story loses its energy and fizzles. The hero and the fan becoming one satisfies self-actualization—the ultimate goal of branding.

With Maslow's foundational thoughts on understanding consumer psychology and decision-making, we identify brands like Nike and Apple as brands that have fostered cultures with cult-like followings. Both brands focus on the consumer's higher-level needs. Nike has been particularly exemplary, the yellow Lance Armstrong "Livestrong" bracelet being a great example of helping a tribe of loyalists identify themselves. The notion of a wristband as badge caught on quickly. For a while thereafter, wristband collecting became the new bandwagon, created by charities and sports organizations like the Eagles. While wristband collecting became popular, none played to the self-actualized consumer like the Livestrong original did. This product created a community of athletes who touted a *Just Do It* attitude, regardless of the circumstances. Nike has had numerous successful campaigns like this one that focus on customers' esteem needs and desire to belong—both higher level needs.

Apple is another brand that has consistently spoken to the critical few. iPod was the first Apple technology that revealed the brand to the masses. The product's appeal was fashioned in true Apple style: The message was not crafted from the perspective of the product; it came from understanding the individual. The first iPod campaign was one of the best visual interpretations of how music makes us feel. Since we couldn't see the faces of the iPod users, it was easy to project an image of ourselves onto the silhouettes. The iPod itself soon became a badge. The technology fostered an incredible feeling of community and belongingness where users shared their love for music, expression, personal gain, and attention. iPod and the iTunes store fulfilled high-level needs, creating an emotional, cult-like level of brand passion and dedication.

## Fostering Customer Communities

Remember physics class? *An object in motion tends to stay in motion.* Customers are accustomed to riding the energy of their group. Their group guides a great deal of their direction and momentum. The customer becomes addicted to the group and the group's behavior. To remain part of the group, they must participate. "You are what the group says you are," says Maslow. This dynamic creates an enormous amount of unconscious pressure to be sociable. That's why we like to talk. And remember, the most powerful communication between groups happens between acquaintances, not strangers or close friends. *Word-of-mouth marketing is foreign to the dynamics of group conversation because it is forced upon the group; it doesn't happen naturally.*

Architects of successful brands become much more than manufacturers of a product or providers of a service—they are developers of customer communities. It is better to offer a community for your loyalists to speak, and let them finish "decorating" the space. HOGS (Harley Owners Group), Parrot Heads (Jimmy Buffett's fan club), and Trekkies all have come together as groups and have created their own unique and highly identifiable personalities. The best brand architects create these communities not by motivating people, but by building an environment where motivated people are willing to make a maximum contribution.

Communities facilitate communication. Modern civilization is built upon communication. Think about it: Without communication, we might still be sitting around the fire in loincloths, planning the design of our next cave picture. The human species has an inherent need and desire to communicate. We need to talk to others. We need to learn. We need to express and share our thoughts, feelings, experiences, and emotions with friends and family. Isolation is definitely not our cup of tea. Think of the millions of man-hours the human race has spent inventing better ways to communicate: The Guttenberg press; the telegraph; the telephone; fax machines; pagers; cellular phones; the Internet; e-mail. As social creatures, we are addicted to communication.

Maslow had a cautionary question for us all: "Why then do we frequently design organizations to satisfy our need for control and not to maximize the contributions of people?"[7] If only today's word-of-mouth marketing practitioners had heeded his warning, they wouldn't have created systems that attempted to control the dissemination of information. Information control systems may create short-term metrics, but ultimately they destroy the brand's endearment to the customer.

## Be Weird Together and Be Weird No More

We have a need to define ourselves, for ourselves and for others. It's how we survive. We need to be noticed. We believe we'll be noticed by being different. When we find other individuals who share our goals or beliefs, we form groups. The more we have in common with the group, the more we like it. We have an inherent need to communicate with others to avoid isolation and a loss of identity.

Consumers want to be a part of a group that's different to help define their identities, which they want to communicate to the world. Look at cult brands like Star Trek or Harley-Davidson. Their brand evangelists flock to conventions dressed as Klingons or biker rallies looking like bad asses. To the outsider they may look weird or different, but to the participant, they are weird together and therefore, weird no more.

Marketers often ask me, "Can we have a cult brand?" Yes! Thinking and feeling resides in both the transactional (which means they select you based on a transaction in the moment) and relational (where the selecting is based upon how they feel about you). Marketers need to focus on marketing to the transactional mindset and serving the relational customer. *The marketer's job is to set the conditions necessary for the brand's development.* Successful entrepreneurs understand this. They create conditions that attract admirers who not only buy their product or service, but also provide consumers an opportunity to create an experience so enjoyable that they form support groups around the brand. It's no different than Woody Allen's attraction to "the orb" in the movie *Sleeper.*

Powerful brands becomes a badge and can be worn as an easily-read symbol to the world. The anonymous buyer's individual identity becomes synonymous with the group. Because they want to remain in the group, they talk. This unprovoked talk about your brand is the Holy Grail of marketing.

*Both social forces and an individual's needs present the opportunity for creating true "word-of-mouth." This insight allows for new ideas and tools to be explored. Biologically-rooted, our new insight is powerful. Let's turn our attention to the conditions needed to inspire Talk.*

# PART IV

## Seven Principles for Understanding Word-of-Mouth

*These seven principles should be understood by all marketers and business owners to help set the appropriate conditions within your business to increase the chances of your customers talking about your company, products, and services. Cult Brands consciously or unknowingly follow and understand these principles.*

# Introduction

Now that you understand the mechanics behind Talk, we'll turn our attention to the practical application of this research. Remember, as you've already learned, people talk because it benefits them, and it's a naturally-occurring phenomenon. As marketers, we don't want to waste time trying to manipulate talk; rather, we want to invest our time creating something worth talking about. The seven governing principles for inspiring WOM are derived from this basic understanding.

Here are the seven principles:

### 1- The Principle of Integrity
*They know that you know that they know.*

### 2- The Principle of Status
*People share what makes them look good.*

### 3- The Principle of Cool
*Ride in front of the "Cool Wave" or wipe out.*

### 4- The Principle of Groups
*Small groups—the critical few—dictate the large.*

### 5- The Principle of Influence
*Everyone is influential—especially on the Internet.*

### 6- The Principle of Meaning
*People talk about what's meaningful to them.*

### 7- The Principle of Surprise
*People love to share what surprises them.*

Let's begin ...

# 1- The Principle of Integrity
*They know that you know that they know.*

Confusing? Essentially, people know you have an intention, and that you've figured out they know you have an intention. What this means from an advertising standpoint is that they know you're trying to sell them a product, and you are aware they know they're trying to be persuaded. Unless you get very adept at meeting their needs, you're going to encounter a nearly-impenetrable barrier.

Don't think you can deceive them into believing you're not trying to coerce them into buying a product. Even if you think the advertising is solid, they're still going to know. People are much better at detecting deception than at being deceivers.[1]

## The Master Con Game

Intentional manipulation will eventually destroy any relationship. As soon as the deception is discovered, trust—the building block of a relationship—vanishes and the relationship degenerates. In many ways, this is what companies who claim to generate word-of-mouth are doing. The word-of-mouth campaigns are represented as being mutually beneficial. When the money runs out to fund the campaigns, so often does the relationship, and the word-of-mouth dries up or turns to negative talk.

Although we don't advocate the following strategy, as it is a form of deception, it does illustrate the dynamics of entering into a mutually-beneficial relationship with a customer. Remember the movies *The Sting or House of Games?* These two movies let you see how the a "confidence (con) game" plays out. They get the mark (the person they're scamming) to think they're on his side and then swindle him. For the scam to work, the mark must believe the deceiver is acting in his best interest and that it is a mutually-beneficial relationship. While many con scenarios seem too good to be true, people still fall for them because they think they will benefit and because they trust the con artist.

In their book *Road Hustler*, the sociologist Robert Prus and and the anonymous con artist C.R.D. Sharper list five basic steps on the psychology of hustlers in a confidence game:

1- Locate a target;
2- Consolidate oneself with the target;
3- Promote the target's investments in one's enterprise;
4- Obtain possession of target investments; and
5- Cool out the target.[2]

A close look at this list reveals that four out of the five steps involve finding a person and gaining trust. Con men realize that the most important step in selling is gaining someone's favor. In the end, they sell the person a fantasy. Imagine what you can do by applying these principles to a genuine relationship where hustling is not the end game.

Creating trust with customers is the basis for long-term relationships and friendships that will keep them coming back and praising your products. Maslow writes:

> This is on the grounds that any enterprise that wishes to endure over a long period of time and to remain in a healthy and growing state would certainly want a non-manipulative, trusting relationship with its customers rather than the relationship of the quick fleecing, never to see them again.[3]

Creating trust with the customer isn't the result of a single business dealing, but rather the result of beneficial, shared experiences over time.[4] You can't decide one day that you want your customers to trust you; it must start at the beginning of your relationship. Ethics expert Jim Lichtman commented, "In business and in public life today ... the thing you erode away faster than anything else is trust. Once the credibility is gone … you're going to have to work two, three, four times as hard to get it back."[5]

## What the *Principle of Integrity* Means For You

Deceptive and manipulative communication erodes the credibility of the messenger. Consumers have learned to spot self-centered brands, if only on a subconscious level. This understanding requires a distinct shift away from old ideas about the seller/customer relationship. As Maslow wrote:

> The way things stand now, the current conceptions and definitions of salesmen and customer are only slight modifications in principle from that of the snake-oil salesmen and the sucker. The relationship is seen very clearly in the language that is used, which implies that either the customer screws the salesman or the salesman screws the customer, and there is much to talk about who gets screwed, who gets raped, who gets exploited, or who gets taken advantage of. Or, it is as if the customer is sometimes spoken of as a sheep with plenty of blood which is there to be sucked by the smarter mosquitoes or leeches or whatever, in other words, he is simply a host animal who is not respected but who is there only to be used or taken advantage of.[6]

This is exactly what happened with the U.S. release of Dr. Pepper/7-Up's *Raging Cow* energy drink. They recruited people on blogs to talk positively about the product and website. When people found out they were being deceived, the marketing scheme backfired.

A study by Mediaedge:cia cited one visitor who wrote, "This website is FAKE. When you are advertising under false pretenses and not being up front about what you're doing … that isn't just wrong, it's immoral and disgusting."[7] Would you want to buy a product after being tricked in this way?

## HOW TO APPLY
### the *Principle of Integrity* to Your Business

*1-* **Develop trust before you develop tactics.**

What are five ways you can demonstrate you understand your customer so they, in-turn, will have a desire to understand you?

*2-* **Avoid dominating the discussion.**

Are you trying to dominate the discussion with your customers? What aspects of your communication with your customers can you let them control? Remember, word-of-mouth doesn't belong to you anyway; it belongs to the consumer. Think back to the relationships you have with others. People who monopolize conversation usually do so for one or two reasons: A) They are either too nervous to let the conversation lull out of fear that others may say something they don't agree with or that will make them look foolish, or B) They are so self-centered they aren't paying attention to anyone else's need to be heard.

*3-* **Genuinely like your customer.**

If you genuinely like your customers, it will show, and there's a much greater chance the customer will like you and your product, and talk favorably of you to their friends. Aaron Shields, the lead researcher for this book, received a handwritten letter from a Cole Haan salesman telling him how it was good to see him again and if he ever needed anything, to let him know. Suffice to say, Aaron will likely return to buy Cole Haan products from the same salesman!

# 2- The Principle of Status
## *People share what makes them look good.*

This principle relates to the nature of gossip. Both negative and positive information reflect positively on the person conveying the information, as both are useful to decision-making. Negative information is perhaps more useful due to its perception as being highly diagnostic.

Supplying accurate information benefits the conveyer as it confers status. Supplying inaccurate information quickly erodes the reputation of the conveyer. As Alexander Chislenko, a researcher on information and artificial intelligence, commented, "In the current economy, the reputation of a person or organization is of the greatest importance in most social and economic interactions."[1]

## LiveSTRONG Mania

The almighty "yellow bracelets." Livestrong bracelets are on the wrists of people from all ages and all demographics.

What started as an attempt to sell five million bracelets exceeded everyone's expectation. In *USA Today*, Lance Armstrong said he thought they'd be "shooting them at each other for years."[2] Since the May 17, 2004 release date, 55 million bracelets have been sold for $1 each.

This is more than an attempt to support a cause. In its first eight years, the Lance Armstrong Foundation raised $11.5 million for educational and research programs for cancer,[3] an impressive figure, but pale compared to what the bracelet has generated. When the bracelets were scarce, people were paying several times the price on sites like eBay to own one, even though their money was going to the seller rather than the charity the bracelet stood for. As journalist Rob Walker observed in *The New York Times Magazine*:

> Obviously, anyone who was particularly keen on supporting the Lance Armstrong Foundation but couldn't find a bracelet could have simply sent a dollar (or $10) directly to the organization itself. But just as obviously, that would leave the buyer without wearable proof of his or her goodwill.[4]

People wanted to show their support and solidarity with the cause the bright yellow bracelet represented.

Sales were steady initially; however, after Armstrong and his team wore them in the 2004 Tour de France, sales went through the roof. Then, runners like Justin Gatlin and Hicham El Guerrouj wore the bracelets during their Olympic races. Sales topped 300,000 bracelets in one day.[5]

The bracelet quickly became trendy. The idea of a bracelet was adopted by other industries, ranging from medicine to business. They were a sign of solidarity with "the cause," the fight against cancer, and the inspirational idea of overcoming the odds; perhaps more significantly, the bracelet symbolized their solidarity with and inclusion in "the group." David Hesskiel, CEO of Cause Marketing Forum, observed, "One of the reasons why bracelets are so successful is that people not only want to support good causes, but they also want to proclaim they're doing that."[6]

You've probably never seen anyone try to cover up his or her bracelet. They're bright, they're meant to be seen, and people want to display them; it makes them look good.

## Scarcity Generates Talk: The Cascading Tulip Craze

People are attracted to rarity because it confers status to its owner. This applies to diamonds or automobiles as well as to information, ideologies, or technology; the rarer, the better. People are more attracted to something when its benefits offer a distinct, appealing alternative to their "everyday lives." If you offer a brand in a distinct way, people will be more attracted to it and will be more likely to talk about it.

What item of rare beauty would be so esteemed that its value would equal the sum of four tons of wheat, eight tons of rye, eight oxen, eight swine, twelve sheep, 126 gallons of wine, 1,080 of beer, 504 gallons of butter, 1,000 pounds of cheese, a bed, a suit of clothes, and a silver drinking cup?

One Viceroy tulip in the mid 1600s.[7]

Tulips, introduced to Western Europe in the 16th Century, were rare and their bulbs were fragile. This scarcity turned them into symbols of social status, leading many people to sell off large portions of their estate to buy one bulb.

The phenomenon rocketed through the upper classes into the middle class, and even among the merchants and shopkeepers. The craze moved beyond the individual and drew the masses.[8] The journalist James Surowiecki writes:

> In cascades ... a few influential people—either because they happened to go first, or because they have particular skills and fill particular holes in people's social networks—determine the course of the cascade. In a cascade, people's decisions are not made independently, but are profoundly influenced—in some cases even determined—by those around them.[9]

The scarcity of the tulip sucked in upper class individuals, creating a fervor of epidemic proportions because of the power and status the symbol conferred.

People are much more inclined to be attracted to something when its benefits offer something very distinct to their everyday lives.

## What the *Principle of Status* Means for You

People are more interested in themselves than you. When they talk, they want to be the center of attention or derive some other benefit. Trying to make them talk about *you* makes you the center of attention. Encouraging them to only say good things erodes their credibility. Additionally, the perception of scarcity increases the value of what is coveted and is more likely to be talked about.

## HOW TO APPLY
### the *Principle of Status* to Your Business

*1-* **Leave the consumers alone.**

Don't put words in their mouth. Don't bribe them to be your messenger.

*2-* **Find ways to let the consumer take credit for finding you, not the other way around.**

Stop making them feel like they are "targets." There is a better chance that they will become brand evangelists if allowed to do so of their own free will.

*3-* **Remain distinctly different.**

If you can highlight your differences, your business will prosper. Compromise or appealing to the masses never leads to distinction. There are always plenty of reasons why we can't be the best we should be, but those reasons are totally meaningless to the consumer and therefore should never be accepted as reason for our failure to keep discovering new ways to serve the customer.

# 3- The Principle of Cool
## *Ride in Front of the "Cool Wave" or wipe out.*

In our Hypersonic Word-of-Mouth World, the search for *cool* is becoming elusive, and when cool becomes "cool," it's not cool for long. Moreover, our technologically-warping world is shortening our cycles of cool.

To understand what is cool, one must know what is *not* cool; you can learn this by listening to your customer. In order to be on top, you must know what's cool before it becomes cool. Just like a wave, if you jump on too late, you're not going to catch it.

## Cool ... It Isn't Just for Teens

On February 19, 1964, a major event in television history took place: The Beatles made their American television debut on the Ed Sullivan Show; they were followed by a magician named Fred Kaps. Fred Kaps was regarded by magicians as the greatest all-around magician (someone who can perform many different types of magic) who ever lived. He won the top prize at an international magic competition (called FISM) three times, more than anyone before or since. His performance was flawless. Yet, if you talked to anyone who saw the show when it originally aired, I'm guessing they'd only mention The Beatles. As mythology expert Joseph Campbell wrote about The Beatles, "Somehow, they were in perfect tune with their time. Had they turned up thirty years before, their music would have fizzled out."[1] Kaps, on the other hand, was not.

Had The Beatles come along later, they likely wouldn't have achieved the status they did. Had they formed their group in 1964 (the year they were on the Ed Sullivan Show), they probably wouldn't have caught on either. In order to be on top, you must know what's cool before it's cool. Just like a wave, if you jump on too late, you're not going to catch it. The Beatles jumped on at just the right time.

In his book *The Tipping Point*, Malcolm Gladwell makes an exciting observation: Little things can make a big difference. However, there's a big problem with current marketing technology: We can't measure the little things. Quantitative data like demographics tell us where the customers are but not where they're going. Most companies find themselves at "the tipping point," and if you are at the tipping point, you've missed it.

The fact that America has 72 million teens doesn't reveal what those 72 million teens buy. We need more relevant information, like an understanding of the stage of life they're in, or how they're choosing products.

Latinos have become the largest minority in the United States. A plethora of statistics prove this, yet we have very little understanding about this minority group. For instance, not all Latinos are Mexicans. Not all Mexicans work the land. Today, most marketing efforts to the Hispanic market are laughable.

"Cool" is not only for teens. Adults also want to be cool. *Cool* is what your social group finds amazing and delightful. Adults share the basic human need to belong to the group of their choosing. Within this group, they want to be cool or, more accurately, to be accepted for their choices. And it is not good enough to belong. Once we belong, the search is on to stand out or "show off," which makes the hunt for cool very elusive. Once you identify the "cool," the wave will likely have passed by the time you go to market.

What is defined as "cool" today is often revealed by yesterday's ignored "uncool." Today, video game players enjoy all the wonderful 3D graphics we only dreamed about as children. But what are they playing? The old Nintendo games like Super Mario Brothers. What is cool today is to play vintage games.

Cool arises from the repressed side of the collective social consciousness. American society once repressed the use of alcohol through prohibition, as the "spirit" seemed to be evil. This same "spirit" is free flowing today in Jimmy Buffett concerts and bars across America. Today, African-American music like rap and hip-hop is cool, and the major fans of their music are white suburban kids who enjoy hearing about hardships they don't have.

## Ignored Today, Cool Tomorrow

Slowly, consumers are getting tired of companies "making" them consume their products without considering their wants, and consumers are taking this to the big screen. In the movie *Super Size Me*, McDonald's—the restaurant that was once a coveted birthday-party place for children—was attacked, along with the unhealthy standards of the fast food industry. McDonald's quickly responded with a healthier menu that included more low-carb, low fat choices. Interestingly, this "consumer demand" for healthier foods was ignored for twenty years.

To discover tomorrow's "cool," look for the voices that are being neglected, suppressed, or ignored. These voices hold clues to what will eventually become "cool."

My mother has experienced this several times in her lifetime. She often exclaims, "I had stuff just like that. I can't believe it's back!" But believe it. What's cool cycles through time. Old ideas re-emerge with new energy, and as time passes, these ideas find a new group.

You can say that when an idea was first born, it filled a need for a certain group of people. When the need was satisfied, the idea was forgotten. For example, the "need" to rebel in the '60s made the Volkswagon Beetle the car of choice. Today, the Beetle has made a comeback as the car of choice for those who rebel against "The Man" in our overly-corporate world. The idea behind the product remains: The VW Beetle is still the little car that is different and stands out, representing the timeless feelings of a restless culture that is constantly looking for more freedom.

To be "in the trend," you must really know your customers, not as demographics, but *as people who want something from you*. Give them what they want but don't expect to receive. Become an "inventor" of cool: Anticipate what they never thought was possible and then deliver it.

## What the *Principle of Cool* Means for You

If you want to be *in*, you have to be part of *cool*. You have to anticipate the tipping point (catch the wave) to take advantage of a trend.

Steve Jobs of Apple Computer says:

> You can't just ask customers what they want and then try to give that to them. By the time you get it built, they'll want something new ... If we'd given customers what they said they wanted, we'd have built a computer they have been happy with a year after we spoke to them— not something they want now.[2]

## HOW TO APPLY
### the *Principle of Cool* to Your Business

*1-*  **Find "cool" clues.**

The clues to what will be cool tomorrow are hiding in what is not cool today. Spend time "futuring"—project your industry into the future to see where the trends might be leading you. Remember that history tends to repeat itself—chart a trend analysis of what's cool as a way of predicting what we may be cycling into next.

*2-*  **Uncover the customer's upcoming unfulfilled needs.**

Cool fulfills a need, but once that need is filled, it is ignored. Fortunately, just below the surface of a fulfilled need lies the next unfulfilled need.

# 4- The Principle of Groups
*Small groups—the critical few—dictate the large.*

Customers can be broken down into two subgroups:

1- The trivial many.
2- The critical few.

Avoid focusing on the *trivial many* and find your brand's *critical few*. They are the ones who truly influence their subculture. The same principle that applies to individuals applies to groups: You need the influence of many small groups to create a cascade.

## Embracing the Critical Few

Cultural anthropologist Margaret Mead once said, "Never doubt that a small group of committed citizens can change the world. Indeed, it is the only thing that ever has." The same is true about product popularity. Malcolm Gladwell aptly termed this phenomenon the "Law of the Few."[1] He writes, "That is the paradox of the epidemic: that in order to create one contagious movement, you often have to create many small movements first."[2]

The economist Vilfredo Pareto came up with the now-famous 80/20 Rule: Twenty percent of all actions induce eighty percent of all outcomes—the law of the trivial many and the critical few. The critical few are those who truly influence their subcultures.

After spending hundreds of hours around the Harley-Davidson community both observing and working for the brand, it was clear to me that the vast of majority of riders are not outlaws. In fact, most of them have "day jobs" jobs like running airlines, law firms, or county governments or they're teachers, doctors, or landscapers. They are the critical few who shaped the bad-boy image of Harley-Davidson. They all wanted a certain degree of "bad-assness" bestowed upon them via their association with the brand. The Harley-Davidson brand represents an escape from their present reality and a safe return. Harley-Davidson is known for saying they don't build bikes, they build dreams.

The same is true of the legions of Parrot Heads who pledge their loyalty to Jimmy Buffett: Few actually live the completely carefree lifestyle. This pattern repeats itself in every community and every culture. Every product or service has a critical few that embraces the brand wholeheartedly.

What applies to individuals applies to groups: Many small groups are needed to create a cascade. These groups, as sociologist Duncan Watts puts it, must make a "trade-off between local stability and global connectivity."[3] In other words, social networks that are poorly connected cannot diffuse information properly, and those that are too highly connected experience no flux because the sheer number of people influencing any single individual.

A study by the late social psychologist Solomon Asch involving the observation of lines has important implications for behavior. Individuals were presented with a group of three lines, each line having a distinct length. They were to identify the line from the group that was equal in size to the test line. In control groups, people always answered correctly. Under experimental conditions, an individual was placed in a group where everyone else was instructed to choose the wrong line. Seventy-five percent of the individuals changed their answer at least once in the direction of the majority.[4]

Asch noted that the results were highly-influenced by individual differences, and the reason for people intentionally choosing the wrong line was not the result of any single pressure.[5] An individual with a lot of independence and status placed with a contrasting group is much less likely to change her mind than an easily-influenced individual placed in a group, especially if the group contains highly-influential individuals. Experimental results are, therefore, likely to vary depending on the dissenter/majority dynamics. Some people are more easily influenced than others.

## Influencing Product Decisions

This study seems to indicate that some individuals will be virtually impossible to influence. This is not true, however, because in making product decisions, most people are looking to be influenced, even if they don't realize it. This concept goes back to economist Herbert Simon's idea of bounded rationality—people are often unable to make decisions on their own due to lack of knowledge. Efficient selection requires an individual to have both general knowledge and specific information.[6] Most people know generally what they are looking for, but lack the specific information they need to make a purchase. This is where they turn to other people for help, especially those they know who have expertise or connections to someone with expertise. It's like asking the servers in restaurants what they recommend, because the server has specialized knowledge about the food.

The influential individuals have it easy—they get to do what they enjoy: Talking to people about something they enjoy. Your job is to get them talking.

## Teenagers: A New Breed of Humans (and a Source of Never-Ending Influence)

Teens rule. Do not ignore them because they don't fall within your target demographic; when you're not looking, they will eat you alive. They are more Internet-savvy than their parents. They know how to find information, and their parents ask their teens' opinions about purchasing decisions because they are so well-connected to information. In many respects, teens are both the gatekeeper and the bridge to influencing your customer.

The problem with understanding the emerging teen culture today is that there's more to them than you'd expect with an ordinary generation gap. As marketers, we believe that if we can understand or experience the teen lifestyle, we would better-understand this new emerging generation of "consumers." But the separation is a cultural abyss so enormous that it is almost as if young people today are from a different planet, both physically and psychologically.

The teen world enjoys access to information at the click of a mouse, and a smorgasbord of experiences and opportunities for the taking. We can no longer pretend to "track" teens' behavior and understand how they affect their parents. These parents unconsciously transferred the freedom of the '60s to their children, who have the courage to act it out. "This is my world and I can experience it the way I want it," they believe, and they're right. Money isn't impressive and the ideas of luxury don't fit their worldview. A Rolex is for "old geezers" who cling too much to their jobs and their junk.

Consider the rise in popularity of mp3 parties, where each person shares their music with the crowd. You can start to see this general attitude of *our world, our way* that has taken over and invaded our most cherished ideas in marketing.

Teens are the gatekeepers of your customer's sphere. Their opinions dictate what is cool and what is out. When they become adults, they're going to be the biggest spenders. They've got influence on the Internet: Teens share their opinions and they've got every reason to talk as it helps them establish and understand their identities.

Teens want to be involved. They're not interested in being inundated by thousands of ads. They want to share their opinions, they want customization, they want the freedom to change their minds, and they want to try products before they buy them.[7]

In their first year of offering custom-fit jeans and chinos online, Lands' End reported that 40 percent of its chinos and jeans sales were customized; they also revealed that the retention rate on customers purchasing custom products was 39 percent higher than their other customers.[8] In 2004, a study by Telecomy, a UK research group, discovered that 85 percent of children had customized their phones.[9] Other retailers have jumped on the bandwagon: You can now customize everything from M&M's to Heinz ketchup bottles.

## Taking Down the KKK

If asked to imagine the defeat of the Klu Klux Klan, you'd probably imagine a federal task force mounting a large-scale effort, or perhaps a civil rights group launching a nationwide campaign. Picture instead a group of children playing.

In the 1940s, in the midst of a nationwide Klan revival, Stetson Kennedy joined the KKK. Kennedy wasn't a man of influence. He was a "regular guy" who regretted not serving his country in World War II, and he was tired of the bigotry of the KKK.[10] He joined the Klan hoping to gain "insider information" that he could report to the government to destroy any chance of a Klan revival.

He contacted the assistant attorney general of Georgia with information about a planned attack on a union rally; he wrote the governor of Georgia with information that could revoke the Klan's non-profit and non-political charter. He was unsuccessful despite all his efforts.[11]

Frustrated, Kennedy started looking for other ways he could exert influence. One day, he saw a group of children playing and began to devise a plan to use a children's show to turn public opinion against the KKK.[12] He contacted the producers of the *Adventures of Superman* radio show and proposed a series of episodes in which Superman would fight the KKK, and secret insider KKK codes and information would be revealed.[13] They were more than happy to oblige.

After the episode aired, children began playing games of Superman vs. the KKK, wearing Klan-like gear, using the Klan's secret codes and handshakes. The Klan members' own children began innocently role-playing in front of their parents.[14]

The Klan was furious; they felt mocked and weakened. They quickly changed their codes, and heard them aired in the next episode.[15] The next time Kennedy went to a meeting, the room was almost empty.[16] And it spread across the country.

By doing things they naturally do—picking up new information and playing games—children crushed the KKK revival.

## What the *Principle of Groups* Means For You

You cannot be all things to all people and expect to have passionate brand evangelists. *You need to build a brand that the critical few can love instead of a brand that the trivial many won't hate.* Don't chase numbers, chase passion.

And in the Hypersonic Word-of-Mouth World, we must show respect for teenagers—not just elders. Kids today are more mature because they are exposed to much more than we were. We can't outsmart them because they live in a networked world 24/7. As marketers, we take "field trips" to experience the fascinating sights and sounds of the wired world, assuming we know everything that goes on there. We shouldn't kid ourselves: We don't live in it like they do.

## HOW TO APPLY
the *Principle of Groups* to Your Business

1- **Look for ways to become something worth talking about.**

Listen to the voices of the few and create something of value for them. Show genuine interest in the critical few who will fall on their swords for you.

2- **Observe teen behavior's role conflict.**

Teens are torn between how their parents, schools, and job markets see them and how they see themselves. Create ways for them to use your brand to define themselves. It will give them the opportunity to elevate the self-image to which they aspire.

3- **Create intrigue and surprise around your brand with teenagers in mind.**

They may not be able to use your product yet, but they will form an opinion and their opinion can become influential.

4- **Throw out your old timelines—you can't stage a communication launch.**

Teens won't wait for your PR department's press release. Don't wait to give your gift of surprise. The sooner the better if you want to harness their influential powers.

# 5- The Principle of Influence
*Everyone is influential—especially on the Internet.*

Connectivity is central to this principle: Everyone is able to influence people in some way, on some subject. No one can affect people's decisions in every category. Those who provide more useful input gain more status and are more likely to be listened to. As we've heard many times before: Knowledge is power.

## Gladwell's Big Three & Population Size

Influential people aren't only those with a great deal of knowledge. In *The Tipping Point*, Malcolm Gladwell lists three categories of people who can create epidemics: Mavens, Connectors, and Salesmen. Mavens are very knowledgeable people who seek knowledge for the sake of knowledge and like to share it. Connectors are influential because of the sheer number of people they can diffuse information to. Salesmen are those that can translate information so that anyone can make sense of it. Gladwell writes, "What Mavens and Connectors and Salesmen do to an idea in order to make it contagious is to alter it in such a way that extraneous details are dropped and others exaggerated so that the message itself comes to acquire a deeper meaning."[1] Maven's are the perfect target for marketers: Connectors and Salesmen need a source of information to disseminate. It's harder to find a better candidate than a knowledge expert.

One critical factor Gladwell's model leaves out, as it is based on biological rather than social epidemics, is that the size of a social group affects an individual's influence. As the size of a social population increases, any individual, regardless of expertise, exerts less influence because there is more information to compete with.[2] Consider movie reviews: You're much more likely to believe a negative review if it's coupled with only two positive reviews than if it's one among forty positive reviews. *The size of the population influences the information.*

What this means is that you can't expect a Maven or two to yield widespread influence. Influential people are best-situated to influence populations of moderate size, and it is the collective influence of all these groups put together that has wide-reaching implications.

## A Passion for Wine

Although the name Robert M. Parker, Jr. probably draws a blank for most of you, for anyone interested in wine, the name conjures up an array of associations—good or bad, depending on what side of his pen you landed on. Parker is "the Michael Jordan of wine tasting";[3] his palate is treated as "the equivalent of Einstein's brain."[4] He is the most influential critic in the world—not just the most influential critic in the wine industry, but the most influential critic in *any* industry.

Powered by passion and hard work, Robert Parker, a small-town boy from Monkton, Maryland, had his first glass of wine in France because the price of Coca-Cola was too high.[5] He went on to transform the wine industry. His language and point system for rating wines is now used almost universally, and he challenged winemakers to improve their methods. Like him or not, since Robert Parker came on the scene, the quality of wine has undisputedly improved.

Parker entered an era that was retreating from the perception of wine as the drink of the upper class. Americans were beginning to understand that anyone could appreciate wine, regardless of his or her background.[6] The industry was largely dominated by the British, many of whom had a financial interest in wine sales.[7] Their criticisms were meant to sell more wine. Newspapers in America picked up on the trend and the critics (who often had little knowledge of the subject) employed by these papers were often secretly encouraged by people looking for monetary gain to promote their wines.

The consumer lacked an advocate before Robert Parker came along. Believing that more critical reviews were needed for wine lovers, Parker began publishing *The Wine Advocate* in 1978. This publication made it easier for the consumer to understand wines: He developed a one-hundred-point system for rating the wine that mirrored standard academic tests, and moved away from the elitist language writers were using to communicate sensory descriptions based on the wine's taste and smell. He related the aromas of wine to actual smells, rather than a romance novel, which meshed with the "wine for everyman" attitude springing up in America.

*The Wine Advocate* grew steadily until 1982. Parker championed the 1982 vintage from the Bordeaux region of France (one of the most well known and respected wine regions in the world). While other reviewers were giving mild and hesitant reviews, Parker declared them "some of the greatest wines of the century."[8] Parker was championed by wine shops and consumers who were looking for an unbiased perspective.

When the vintage was released, Parker was right: It was superb. His influence skyrocketed and his reputation grew. Today, his reviews can make or break a wine. As James McInerney, reporter for the *New York Times* wrote, "A single point on his rating scale can be worth hundreds of thousands of dollars to a winemaker."[9]

He has been widely criticized and not everyone agrees with his reviews. He has even received death threats and lawsuits. But, Parker is committed to serving the consumer.

## A World of Bloggers

Parker's rise to wine stardom is a great metaphor for the rise of marketing on the Internet. No one could have predicted the power one individual would come to wield in the wine industry—in the same way no one could have predicted the power of blogging. In *Wired* magazine, Kevin Kelly, the founding executive editor, explained:

> No Web phenomenon is more confounding than blogging. Everything media experts knew about

audiences—and they knew a lot—confirmed the focus
group belief that audiences would never get off their
butts and start making their own entertainment …
Blogs and other participant media would never
happen, or if they happened, they would not draw
an audience, or if they drew an audience they would
not matter.[10]

How wrong they were. The Web gave the consumer a voice and
blogging made it easy and convenient to be heard. Data about
consumers failed to reveal their motivations; focus groups said they
were lazy. What the focus groups should have revealed was that they
didn't have the power to publish. Lacking this power to publish,
consumers were forced to listen to traditional media and talk about it
with a few friends. Blogging gave them a platform in front of the
world. And, without the inhibitions of face-to-face communication,[11]
people were willing to speak their minds.

Bernard Cohen's statement that the press "may not be successful
much of the time in telling people what to think, but it is stunningly
successful in telling them what to think *about*"[12] remains just as true
today as it was in 1963, with one exception: The public has gotten
more powerful in telling itself what to think. Readers and viewers have
become hesitant to trust the "objectivity" of mainstream media,
favoring instead those who proudly offer their opinion. It seems much
more relevant to hear, "Microsoft sucks and this is why," than, "Public
opinion on Microsoft is down ten percent."

Consumers want what Parker was to the wine industry: They want
opinions from an unbiased source in a language they can understand.
They are more inclined to trust bloggers because it is harder for them to
deceive someone about their viewpoint. As blogger Rebecca Blood
notes, for people publishing everyday, without an editor, if they're fak-
ing, they're bound to slip up and someone's bound to notice.[13]

Companies have started to realize the power of the individual voice. When we went to press, if you searched Google for "Robert," the number one return is someone you probably couldn't have guessed: Blogger Robert Scoble.[14] Scoble is employed by Microsoft and they let him blog about anything he wants, good or bad. This lack of filtering is crucial to his popularity.

Other companies have attempted to start their own blogs, but are usually sterilized by legal departments that remove any trace of personality. Worse still are blogs designed by corporations to trick customers, like Dr. Pepper did when they created a Raging Cow website and hired people to blog about it for them. With the number of consumers surfing the Web, any attempt to trick or deceive fails— the consumer has become Big Brother and many companies are learning the hard way.

It is becoming easier and easier for people to control what they listen to, watch, and read. With the advent of RSS (Really Simple Syndication)—a web-feed format that enables programs to search and organize the feeds for users—people can have their news filtered for them; the feeds deliver only what they are interested in, putting the consumer in control of what he or she sees and hears.

This has opened the door for more experts. Traditional means of credibility, like degrees or social standing, are circumvented by the faceless Internet. Where encyclopedias were previously the domain of the cognoscenti, they are now the domain of "The Man in the Basement." Jim Wales's *Wikipedia* has become the biggest encyclopedia on the planet, open for contributions from anyone. The monitoring and policing of quality is pretty astounding:

> When MIT's Fernanda Viégas and IBM's Martin Wattenberg and Kushal Dave studied Wikipedia, they found that cases of mass deletions, a common form of vandalism, were corrected in a median time of 2.8

minutes. When an obscenity accompanied the mass deletion, the median time dropped to 1.7 minutes.[15]

Wikipedia and the blogs have many detractors who claim that the writers aren't qualified to deliver the content. But the detractors' voices are being muffled: The lines between mainstream media and consumer-controlled content are slowly blurring. Online newspapers are inviting readers to participate in blogs on the newspapers' websites, acting as "citizen-journalists."[16] When University of Michigan professor Juan Cole had trouble publishing his ideas, he started a blog that lead to an appearance on CNN as an expert.[17] And *Time Magazine* even called blogs "a genuine alternative to mainstream news outlets."[18]

When Dan Rather slipped up on national television, it wasn't the mainstream media that first became suspicious, it was bloggers. And it wasn't mainstream media that first revealed the folly, it was the blog *Powerline.com*.[19]

Tired of the often cold, emotionless mainstream reports of September 11, many turned to blogs to hear about the other side—the personal stories. It showed the side the media wouldn't touch. As journalist Nick Denton wrote, "Only through the human stories of escape or loss have I really felt the disaster … These stories … have a rude honesty that does not make its way through the mainstream media's good-taste filter."[20]

Blogs are sprouting up at an astronomical rate: According to Technorati, a blog search engine, everyday 175,000 new blogs are created and 1.6 million posts are made; their database currently holds 60 million blogs.[21]

Although most of these blogs will disappear into oblivion, remember the next Robert M. Parker, Jr. could be out there buying your products.

## What the *Principle of Influence* Means For You

Influential people only exist within a category. Influential people tend to be much more aware of the scope of their influence, which is typically limited to the area(s) in which they specialize. They are hard to manipulate. They are, as a study by Mediaedge:cia explained, "heavy users," "more aware of brands," "have used more brands," and are "more motivated by brand and less by price."[22]

Being such highly-interested people, the products they use play a major role in their lives. A brand's identity is reflected in its major users, and is especially significant to its most loyal users. They don't want to purchase products that are contradictory to the image they desire to project. This is where traditional advertising is helpful: It sends a message that resonates with the lifestyles of the brand loyalists.

## HOW TO APPLY
the *Principle of Influence* to Your Business

*1-*   **Influence many small groups of influencers.**

This is perhaps the best way to achieve the most widespread results.

*2-*   **Stay relevant to your customer.**

Useful information is the highest form of currency, so always find ways to provide useful knowledge to your customer.

*3-*   **Respect your audience.**

Since you can't control who talks, you must respect all who may be listening. Anyone is capable of carrying your brand's torch or burning you to the ground. Respect the power of the individual.

# 6- The Principle of Meaning
## *People talk about what's meaningful to them.*

Listen carefully to your customers to find out what the critical few care about—then give them something to talk about. If you can find ways to amuse them, surprise them and provide them with information that will confirm their own self-images and give them worth among their peers, they will talk. And others will follow.

## The Rise of *El Ñato*

A while back, I posted a sampling from an up-and-coming reggaeton artist named *El Ñato Bellaco* on two music forums. One was for reggaeton enthusiasts and the other was a general discussion group. *El Ñato's* lyrics were absurd, his voice was far from attractive, and he didn't even exist. On the reggaeton forum, feedback started to flow. Some loved it and most hated it, but everyone wanted to listen to *El Ñato*. They gave him tips to improve his music and passed it on to others who love reggaeton. In a matter of hours, *El Ñato's* song had been heard by more than one hundred people, including a famous reggaeton artist in Puerto Rico. Within hours, he had affected an entire community of reggaeton-lovers.

On the general music discussion forum, not a single person responded. They didn't care. *El Ñato* only had influence within the community that embraced his passion and love for reggaeton. The experiment only worked on the reggaeton website because those people cared about their music.

In *The Open Door*, Peter Brook, perhaps the greatest living theater director and theorist, described a very interesting occurrence in Iran.[1] When he went to an Iranian village in 1970, he saw a form of theater called the *Ta'azieh*. The *Ta'azieh* is the Islamic equivalent to a mystery play—a type of theater that rose out of religious theater in Europe in the Middle Ages and introduced apocryphal elements into biblical stories, generating the disapproval of the church. It is deeply rooted in tradition. Describing the event, Brook wrote:

> I became aware of a low murmur all around me, and taking my eyes for a moment off the action, I saw lips trembling, hands and handkerchiefs stuck in mouths, faces wrought with paroxysms of grief and the very old men and women, then the children and then the young men on bicycles all began sobbing freely. Only our tiny group of foreigners remained dry-eyed.[2]

A year later, a *Ta'azieh* was performed at the Shiraz International Festival of the Arts. People from surrounding villages were brought together and dressed in costumes to present the audience with the best *Ta'azieh* possible. The spectators were happy to see the performance, but the response was nowhere close to impact the *Ta'azieh* had in the village a year before.

What would cause such a radically different response between villagers and foreigners to a play? As Brook so elegantly puts it: "Because the meaning of the *Ta'azieh* starts not with the audience at the performance, but with the way of life experienced by that audience."[3]

The same thing that was true for *El Ñato* and the *Ta'azieh* is true for advertising and products: *What has meaning for one group will be irrelevant to another group.* As a marketer, you need to figure out a way to get your message to stick.

Gladwell writes, "The hard part of communication is often figuring out how to make sure a message doesn't go in one ear and out the other."[4] We'd say the hard part isn't figuring out how to make it stick— that's the easy part. You just need to tap into what people care about. Figuring out what they care about is the hard part.

"The fact that Mavens want to help for no other reason than because they like to help, turns out to be an awfully effective way of getting someone's attention."[5] *Find out what the core users care about, and make sure to target them with your product and message.* Everyone else will follow.

## Mormon Mania

One of the most powerful forces in the world has always been religion. Barbara Hargrove, professor of the sociology of religion at Iliff School of Theology, described new religions (or "cults") as the result of feeling unfulfilled by one's mainstream religious upbringing. The void left by mainstream religion resulted in the formation of two types of religion: Transformative and integrative.

Transformative religions arise in response to feelings that the current system is too rigid, and presents a system that is much more flexible. Integrative religions arise in response to a need for structure, leading to religions with distinct hierarchies and cues to determine insiders from outsiders.[6] By opposing themselves to conventional practices, these religions offer a distinct alternative to fill the "void" in people's lives.

The Mormons started as a cult but achieved mainstream status. Their ideas were offered as an alternative to mainstream values: They sanctioned polygamy, although few Mormons practiced it. They established a theocratic government that made every man into a priest and that attempted to bypass the American government's authority and economic system. Though they were persecuted, they relentlessly promoted their "radical ideas." Laurence Moore, director of the Cardiff Institute of Society, Health and Ethics, writes:

> In noting these problems that beset efforts to make out an 'objective' case for Mormon difference, we arrive finally at a less complex proposition: Mormons were different because they said they were different

and because their claims frequently advanced in the most obnoxious way possible, prompted others to agree and to treat them as such. The notion of Mormon difference, that is, was a deliberate invention elaborated over time … One result of the conflict was an ideology that sought to turn the self-advertised differences of the Mormons into a conspiracy against the American public.[7]

This encouragement of the "rhetoric of deviance" helped them to establish a distinct identity and contributed significantly to their long-term success. What they offered was different, clearly distinct, and, therefore, attractive.

## What the *Principle of Meaning* Means for You

Put simply, don't focus on ways to control the conversation; focus on ways to get it started.

# HOW TO APPLY
## the *Principle of Meaning* to Your Business

*1-* **Create magnetic ideas with greater meaning.**

Since it is consumers who build brands, it is the job of the marketer to create magnetic ideas that will make them want to talk and care about what we offer.

*2-* **Have a cause.**

Find more new ways to make them care.

*3-* **Embrace the element of surprise.**

Find new ways to surprise, delight, and serve your customer. Always look for new ways to surprise. *(See The Principle of Surprise.)*

# 7- The Principle of Surprise
*People love to share what surprises them.*

Never underestimate the power of surprise. Have you considered letting the consumer discover the best thing about you instead of shouting it from the rooftops?

## Frog Prince Marketing

See if you recognize this story: A princess is walking along a lake, playing with her prized golden ball. The ball slips from her hands and falls into the lake. A prince approaches her and offers to retrieve the ball if she will promise to love him. Thinking she will easily escape after he gets her ball, she tells him she will. The prince dives into the lake, retrieves the ball, and returns it to the princess who quickly runs away. Later that evening, the prince knocks on the castle door. When the princess sees it is the prince, she slams the door in his face and returns to her seat at the dinner table. Not one to let a few cheek splinters stop him, the prince waits for an opportune time to ask the princess for a kiss. She finally agrees and immediately falls in love, realizing he is the man of her dreams. They get married and live happily ever after.

Do you recognize this version of *The Frog Prince*? Probably not, because in this version, the prince is always a prince and the storyline is pretty unremarkable. You probably wouldn't remember it or repeat it to anyone—there's nothing amusing, surprising, or special about it.

*You're probably wondering what this has to do with marketing?* The majority of marketing attempts to sell products pragmatically, as is, or attempts to oversell it. In other words, marketers present the products as if the products are "princes." Once the consumer gets the product, they find out the product is either a prince (if it does exactly what it's supposed to do) or it's a frog (when it doesn't meet the hype). If the product delivers what it's supposed to, there's no reason for anyone to talk about it. The consumer would only be repeating what someone else has already said. Theinformation isn't useful, and it won't help someone's status. If the product turns out to be a frog, people will talk negatively about it because they will feel deceived. They will make sure other people know how disappointing the product is, and gain status for providing the information.

People don't like to be deceived unless they're getting something better than what they expected. Famed sociologist Erving Goffman wrote:

> When a disclosure shows that we have been participating with a performer who has a higher status than he has led us to believe, there is a good Christian precedent for our reacting with wonderment and chagrin rather than hostility. Mythology and our popular magazines, in fact, are full of romantic stories in which the villain and the hero both make fraudulent claims that are discredited in the last chapter, the villain proving not to have a high status, the hero proving not to have a low one.[1]

When people find they are getting more value than they expected, they won't hold it against you—they'll praise you. This is exactly what happens in the Frog Prince story. The princess gets more than she expected. Instead of the frog being a frog, it turns out to be a prince. Part of the reason we enjoy telling the story is *we like our expectations to be exceeded*. Therefore we must set conditions that allow us to exceed expectations.

Let me repeat: *If your product lives up to your hype, there's no reason for people to talk about it* (as happened when the prince turned out to be a prince). If your product doesn't meet the hype, people will talk about it negatively (like when the prince turned out to be a frog). If it's a good product and it exceeds the hype, people will rave about it, because the frog has turned out to be a prince!

You need people to talk about your product so information about the product will spread to different social groups. If people don't know about it or don't know that it's valuable, there's no reason for them to buy it. Adam Fogelson, head of marketing for Universal Pictures, commented, "I don't think simply a satisfying version of what someone expects will guarantee a great box office."[2] Although people aren't going to complain about being satisfied, they're not going to write home about it either.

## Negative WOM Spreads Like Wildfire

Don't think you can escape the pitfalls of negative word-of-mouth. In fact, studies have shown that there is a greater chance that negative word-of-mouth will spread wider than positive word-of-mouth. If your product doesn't deliver, you're sunk. Drawing on many of these studies, Kamins, Folkes, and Perner wrote:

> Negative (vs. positive) product information is generally perceived as more diagnostic or informative and weighed more heavily in consumer judgments … Negative (vs. positive) opinions are also more likely to be attributed to the product rather than to the transmitter, giving the opinion more credibility … Further, stories about product flaws may be more vivid and accessible from memory during conversations … facilitating transmittal.[3]

When people complain about the faults of products, they are diffusing some of the anger they feel about being deceived. People don't like to be deceived. No one wants to purchase a car, only to find out it's a lemon.

This is exactly what happened to Apple with their failed Newton, one of the early PDAs. It didn't come close to meeting the hype. As Ed Coolligan of Palm Pilot put it, "They over-promised and under-delivered."[4] This was the complete opposite of the mantra that carried

Jeff Hawkins, Donna Dubinsky, and Ed Colligan from Palm to Handspring, helping them turn the handheld business into a billion dollar industry by "under-promising and over-delivering."[5]

In 1917, British businessman George Smith wrote:

> The cleverest salesman in the world, the best writer of advertisements in the world, cannot, alone, continue to make sales of anything which has not in itself selling merit; and, on the other hand, the worst salesman in the universe, supplemented by the worst copywriter in the universe, cannot avoid making sales of something which has in it the selling idea ... Real selling begins with the conception of the article, goes through every branch of the business, and the salesman should be not a mere individual but the interpreter to the buyer ... Real selling is mutual; it is bringing to a man some thing that he needs or wants ... Selling is not a separate division of business; it is business ... The selling ideas are put in by the factory, and therefore the factory should know the consumer ... The best is that which the public determines to be best.[6]

And they lived happily ever after ...

## Shyamalan's Surprise

Surprise is one of the most effective means of inducing word-of-mouth transmission. A study by psychologists Christian Derbaix and Joëlle Vanhamme found that 78 percent of study subjects reported word-of-mouth transmissions of surprising events, whereas only 28 percent of study subjects reported word-of-mouth transmission of non-surprising events.[7] If people are surprised, it's hard for them not to talk.

Surprise not only affects transmission by the person experiencing the surprise, but also affects secondary transmission by those to whom the surprising event is reported. The more intense an event is to the person experiencing it, the more likely it is that both the person experiencing the event and the person hearing about the event will share it with someone else.[8]

Remember *The Sixth Sense*? Watching the movie's trailer made it look like another horror thriller. It premiered at the end of the summer, a time notorious for bad movies. No one could have guessed what he or she was going to see from the then-virtually-unknown director M. Night Shyamalan. When people saw it, their expectations were shattered. I remember people telling me to see the movie when they hadn't even seen it themselves, just because they heard it was "crazy."

The surprise generated positive word-of-mouth and it reflected at the box office. *The Sixth Sense* went on to generate $293.5 million in the United States. Driven by repeat viewings of people wanting to recapture the surprise induced by the twist ending, the movie had incredible staying power, remaining in theaters for almost a year (from August 1999 through May 2000). It was one of the top ten grossing movies for fifteen weekends in a row, and for the first nine weeks, it had the smallest weekend-to-weekend decline of any movie in the top ten.[9]

Other standard supernatural thrillers like *Stigmata* and *Stir of Echoes* opened while *The Sixth Sense* was at the box office but quickly dropped from the charts. The message is obvious: *Surprise them and they'll pay you back.*

## What the *Principle of Surprise* Means for You

Children love to play hide and seek—there's joy in finding something that's hidden. As we grow up, that longing for surprise never really goes away. We like to discover hidden treasures—it's the stuff that we want to share with others.

## HOW TO APPLY
### the *Principle of Surprise* to Your Business

*1-* **Under-promise and over-deliver.**

Everything but our ego says it's preferable to under-promise and over-deliver.

*2-* **Hide some of your best qualities.**

Avoid revealing everything to the consumers, and find ways to exceed their expectations.

*3-* **Become an idea-generating machine.**

Thomas Edison's goals was to come up with a minor invention every ten days and a major invention every six months. If you want to build a great brand, set similar idea-generation goals. New ideas are scarce. That's why they're so attractive to consumers.

*4-* **Continually find ways to create surprise.**

Never stop at, or rely on, only one good idea. Everyone loves a good idea, and as soon as you come up with one, everyone will copy it. Brands get tired because they fail to continually surprise their customers.

# PART V

*Further insights marketers and business owners can use to better understand their role in today's Hypersonic Word-of-Mouth World*

# LEARNING TO LISTEN

It is the province of knowledge to speak, and it is the privilege of wisdom to listen.

—Oliver Wendell Holmes

Accept your role in the Hypersonic Word-of-Mouth World: *You can't create word-of-mouth; you* CAN *create something worth talking about.* Always remember the primary tenet of *Why We Talk*, which conflicts with most WOM marketing programs: People talk when it benefits them. You can't manipulate this basic truth and build a brand with staying power. Your challenge, then, is to inspire word-of-mouth, enable it, and empower it. How? By listening to your customers.

Freud, Maslow, Jung, and Pavlov have all examined what makes us tick, and though each has a different perspective, they all come to the same basic conclusion: We are all more alike than we are different. This is key to understanding why we talk: We talk because we need to be heard. Acceptance of our perspective elevates our status. Having someone listen to us validates our importance.

We are wired to talk. We do it spontaneously—often without much thought. That's pure word-of-mouth. People talk organically, not mechanically. Any effort to manipulate conversations erodes the integrity of true word-of-mouth.

Talk is powerful, and we will do well to remember that good talking comes from our ability to listen. It is the interpretation and internalization of communication that gives it power. Marketing teams, where the main priority is getting others to talk, are missing the opportunity to *hear the customer.* In the clutter of white papers and fads, we fail to see the customer's life. Sam Walton often told his executives: *If you don't know what to do, go ask the customer. If it's not happening in the store, it's not important.*

The convention that surrounds much of what we attempt to do in marketing is that communication involves talking. Taken to its extreme, it involves dominating the conversation. While we can't argue that talk is powerful, we will remind you that talking comes from our need to be heard. Without a receptive ear, talking has no relevance.

Marketing teams that mistakenly believe the primary objective of marketing is to talk about themselves are forgetting the simple truth that *listening—not talking—is the most powerful component of communication.* The reason this non-talking dynamic is hard for most marketers to grasp is because they don't understand how to create *listening.* Our rush to dominate communication is revealed because we talk before we listen. Or we try to circumvent the listening process by taking disastrous shortcuts. We create research studies full of questions designed to confirm what we want to hear rather than listening for what the consumer really wants to tell us. We don't ask questions that may reveal consumers' uncomfortable answers. This terrible form of censorship hides the truth that we desperately need to listen to.

If you don't think listening is the most powerful form of communication, think about the people you like most. Chances are, you like them because they listen to you. They ask you about yourself. They rarely talk about themselves. *Listening leads to trust, and trust leads to favoritism.*

If someone likes you, your foot is in the door. People make decisions based on what they like and what *feels good* to them emotionally. Most people, however, have a hard time expressing why they feel something (because feelings are based on emotions rather than thoughts), so they attempt to explain and rationalize their feelings using language connected to products and corporate attributes.

The research in my book *The Power of Cult Branding* highlighted the fact that cult brands focus on serving the wants and needs of customers already won. They don't get sucked into the trap of building products and services that might attract new customers. They focus on their brand's existing customers—respecting, valuing, rewarding, and listening to them. Cult brands don't ignore an enthusiastic follower. Remember, core followers all want to believe, but first they need to see "miracles" in the form of unexpected gifts and surprises. Cult brands do extraordinary things for their followers, who in turn become incredible brand evangelists.

*Listening* is the cornerstone of the world's great brands because it leads to the discovery of what will surprise, amuse, and reward your customers. If you want your marketing message to be heard, you have to be willing to listen. Do you trust your customers well enough to enter into a relationship with the soul of your customer?

# REFERENCES

## PART I: OVERVIEW

1  Dunbar, *Grooming, Gossip and the Evolution of Language,* 170.
2  Hawkins, *Truth Vs. Falsehood,* 129-131.
3  Maslow, *Maslow On Management,* 12.

## PART II: A HYPERSONIC WORD-OF-MOUTH WORLD

### The Forces Behind Talk
1  Pandya, *Box Office Guru.*
2  Ibid.
3  Munoz, "High-Tech Word of Mouth."
4  Boyle, "Brand Killers," 92.

### Grunt-of-Mouth Grows Up
1  Standage, *The Victorian Internet,* 50.
2  Neistat, Interview by Neil Cavuto, *Fox News.*
3  Steuver, "Battery and Assault."
4  Neistat and Neistat, *iPod's Dirty Secret.*

### Time Compression: The Need For Speed
1  Mann, "A Remote Control For Your Life," 44.
2  Tchong, *Trendscape 2004,* 15.
3  "Ericsson CEO sees global mobile phone."
4  "Messaging."
5  "Internet Usage Statistics."
6  Kaplan, "Enterprises beware: IM attacks break record again."
7  "U.S. Teens Graduate From Choosing IM Buddy Icons."
8  Tchong, *Trendscape* 2004, 14.
9  Ibid., 44.
10 "Federal Communications Commission Releases Data."
11 Munoz, "High-Tech Word of Mouth."
12 Rosen, *The Anatomy of Buzz,* 17.
13 Nogueira, "Site posts low-tech hack for iTunes giveaway."
14 Smith and Szathmáry, *The Major Transitions In Evolution,* 3 and 6.
15 Kurzweil, "The Law of Accelerating Returns."
16 Rheingold, *The Virtual Community,* 16.

### Media Fragmentation: You Don't Need Mass Media to Inspire Mass Interest
1  Tapscott, *Growing Up Digital,* 3.
2  Ibid., 185.
3  Higgins, *The Art of Writing Advertising,* 12 and 14.
4  Rose, "The Lost Boys," 117.
5  Anderson, "Worst week ever for television ratings."
6  Goetzl, "New Data Reveals Virtually No Viewers."
7  "Adults With Digital Video Recorders Upscale And Print-Oriented."
8  Tchong, 2004, 52.
9  Hoffer, *The True Believer,* 103.

[10] Blackshaw and Nazzaro, "Consumer-Generated Media," 4.
[11] Ibid., 7.

## PART III: AN ANTHROPOLOGICAL, HISTORICAL AND PSYCHOLOGICAL ANALYSIS OF TALK

### Language: The Anatomy of Communication
[1] "Stephen Hawking: … communicating."
[2] Gardner and Gardner, "Teaching Sign Language to a Chimpanzee," 671.
[3] Pinker, *The Language Instinct,* 348.
[4] Leavens and Hopkins, "Intentional Communication by Chimpanzees," 813.
[5] Corballis, *From Hand to Mouth*, 101.
[6] Pinker, T*he Language Instinct,* 32-33.
[7] Fox, "Deaf children reveal how language is born."
[8] Pinker, *The Language Instinct,* 18.
[9] Ibid., 151.
[10] Myers, *Intuition,* 17.
[11] Pinker, *The Language Instinct,* 150.
[12] Ibid., 276.
[13] Corballis, *From Hand to Mouth,* 185.
[14] Ibid., 186-188.
[15] Dunbar, Grooming, Gossip and the Evolution of Language, 168.
[16] Ibid., 170.
[17] Roloff, "Interpersonal Influence," 116.
[18] Kamins, Folkes, and Perner, "Consumer Responses to Rumors," 173.
[19] Ibid.

### Gossip: The Backbone of Word-of-Mouth
[1] Lumley, *Means of Social Control,* 211.
[2] Dunbar, *Grooming, Gossip and the Evolution of Language,* 4.
[3] Nicholson, "The new word on GOSSIP."
[4] Ibid., 42.
[5] Ben-Ze'ev, "The Vindication of Gossip," 15.
[6] Westen, "The Real Slant On Gossip," 46.
[7] Goodman, *Introduction to Good Gossip,* 3.
[8] Goffman, *The Presentation of Self in Everyday Life*
[9] Ben-Ze'ev, "The Vindication of Gossip," 15.
[10] Crowley and Crolwey, *Take Our Word For It,* no. 50.
[11] Dunbar, Grooming, *Gossip and the Evolution of Language,* 79.
[12] Dunbar, "Coevolution of neocortical size," 689.
[13] Corballis, "A gesture in the right direction?," 697.
[14] Latourette, *A History of the Expansion of Christianity,* 164.
[15] Westen, "The Real Slant On Gossip," 47.
[16] Ibid., 80.
[17] Ibid., 46.
[18] Rheingold, *The Virtual Community,* 60.

### Connectedness: The Architecture of Gossip
[1] Travers and Milgram, "An Experimental Study," 430-437.
[2] Milgram, "The Small-World Problem," 65.
[3] Chislenko, "Automated Collaborative Filtering;" Watts, *Six Degrees,* 136.
[4] Granovetter, "The Strength of Weak Ties," 1376.

5  Ibid., 1367.
6  Kleinfeld, "The Small World Problem," 65.
7  Milgram, "The Small-World Problem," 66.
8  Watts, *Six Degrees,* 107.
9  Ibid., 108.
10  Ibid., 116.
11  "Where's Debbie?," 5.
12  Werner and Parmelee, "Similarity of Activity Preferences."
13  Ibid., 62.
14  Dubrovsky, Kiesler, and Sethna, "The Equalization Phenomenon," 119-120.
15  Ibid., 124.

**Social Systems: Where We Talk**
1  Potts, "The chorus line hypothesis."
2  Maslow, *Maslow On Management,* 15.
3  Zyman, *The End of Marketing As We Know It,* 232.
4  Zyman, *The End of Advertising As We Know It,* 189.
5  Ibid.
6  Maslow, *Motivation and Personality.*
7  Maslow, *Maslow On Management,* 11.

## PART IV: 7 PRINCIPLES FOR UNDERSTANDING WORD-OF-MOUTH

### 1. The Principle of Integrity
1  Goffman, *The Presentation of Self In Everyday Life,* 9.
2  Prus and Sharper, *Road Hustler,* 2.
3  Maslow, *Maslow On Management,* 262.
4  Govier, *Dilemmas of Trust,* 32.
5  Levin, "Guarding Your Tongue."
6  Maslow, *Maslow On Management,* 250.
7  "Where's Debbie?," 6.

### 2. The Principle of Status
1  Chislenko, "Automated Collaborative Filtering."
2  Ruibal, "Livestrong shows solidarity of 50M."
3  Ibid.
4  Walker, "Yellow Fever," 23.
5  Layden, "Bracelet mania."
6  Lieber, "Brace yourself."
7  Mackay, *Extraordinary Popular Delusions,* 91.
8  Watts, *Six Degrees,* 205.
9  Surowiecki, *The Wisdom of Crowds,* 57.

### 3. The Principle of Cool
1  Campbell, *The Power of Myth,* 164.
2  Gendron and Burlingham, "The Entrepreneur of the Decade," 116.

### 4. The Principle of Groups
1  Gladwell, *The Tipping Point,* 21.
2  Ibid., 192.
3  Watts, *Six Degrees,* 241.
4  Asch, "Effects of Group Pressure," 154.

5  Ibid., 156.
6  Chislenko, "Automated Collaborative Filtering."
7  Tapscott, *Growing Up Digital,* 187-190.
8  "Lands' End is moving its success in online."
9  Mucha, "Young and Upwardly Mobile."
10  Levitt and Dubner, *Freakanomics,* 58.
11  Ibid., 63.
12  Ibid.
13  Ibid., 63-64.
14  Ibid., 64.
15  Ibid., 65.
16  Ibid.

## 5. The Principle of Influence
1  Gladwell, *The Tipping Point,* 203.
2  Watts, *Six Degrees,* 240.
3  McInerney, *Bacchus & Me,* 165.
4  "Playing the Rating Game," 94.
5  McCoy, "The Emperor of Wine, 12."
6  Ibid., 53.
7  Ibid., 65.
8  Ibid., 104.
9  McInerney, *Bacchus & Me,* 167.
10  Kelly, "We Are the Web," 99.
11  Dubrovsky, Kiesler, and Sethna, "The Equalization Phenomenon," 119-120.
12  Cohen, *The Press and Foreign Policy,* 13.
13  Blood, "weblogs: a history and perspective."
14  Scoble, "Blogs: Humanizing the Face of Corporate America," 132.
15  Pink, "The Book Stops Here," 128.
16  Burstein, "From Cave Painting To Wonkette," xvii.
17  Drezner and Farrell, "Web of Influence," 86-87.
18  Grossman, "Meet Joe Blog," 65.
19  Kline, "Toward A More Participant Democracy," 12.
20  Denton, "Second Sight: The atrocity through the eyes of weblogs."
21  *Technorati.*
22  "Where's Debbie?," 9.

## 6. The Principle of Meaning
1  Brook, *The Open Door,* 44-54.
2  Ibid., 48-49.
3  Ibid., 52.
4  Gladwell, *The Tipping Point,* 24-25.
5  Ibid., 67.
6  Hargrove, "Integrative and Transformative Religions," 260-265.
7  Moore, *Religious Outsiders and the Making of Americans,* 31-32.

## 7. The Principle of Surprise
1  Goffman, *The Presentation of Self In Everyday Life,* 60.
2  Munoz, "High-Tech Word of Mouth."
3  Kamins, Folkes, and Perner, "Consumer Responses to Rumors," 169.
4  Butter and Pogue, *Piloting Palm,* 54.
5  Ibid., 272.

6  Witzel, "Marketing."
7  Derbaix and Vanhamme, "Inducing word-of-mouth by eliciting surprise," 106.
8  Christophe and Rimé, "Exposure to the social sharing of emotion."
9  Pandya, *Box Office Guru.*

# BIBLIOGRAPHY

"Adults With Digital Video Recorders Upscale And Print-Oriented." *Mediamark Research*, July 26, 2006. http://www.mediamark.com/.

Anderson, Nate. "Worst week ever for television ratings." *Ars Technica*, July 21, 2006. http://arstechnica.com/news.ars/post/20060721-7324.html (December 04, 2006).

Asch, Solomon E. "Effects of Group Pressure upon the Modification and Distortion of Judgements." *In Group Dynamics: Research and Theory*, edited by Dorwin Cartwright and Alvin Zander, 151-162. Evanston, IL: Row, Peterson and Company, 1953.

Ben-Ze'ev, Aaron. "The Vindication of Gossip." *In Good Gossip*, edited by Robert F. Goodman and Aaron Ben-Ze'ev, 11-24. Lawrence, KS: University Press of Kansas, 1994.

Blackshaw, Pete, and Mike Nazarrao. "Consumer-Generated Media (CGM) 101: Word-of-Mouth in the Age of the Web-Fortified Consumer." *Intelliseek*, Spring 2004. http://www.intelliseek.com/images/downloads/ISwp_CGM.pdf.

Blood, Rebecca. "weblogs: a history and perspective." *Rebecca's pocket*, September 07, 2000. http://www.rebeccablood.net/essays/weblog_history.html (December 06, 2005).

Boyle, Matthew. "Brand Killers." *Fortune* 148, no. 3 (2003): 88-100.

Brook, Peter. *The Open Door: Thoughts on Acting and Theatre*. New York: Parthenon Books, 1993.

Burstein, Dan. "From Cave Painting To Wonkette: A Short History of Blogging." In *Blog! How the Newest Media Revolution Is Changing Politics, Business, and Culture*, edited by David Kline and Dan Burstein, xi-xxvi. New York: CDS Books, 2005.

Butter, Andrea, and David Pogue. *Piloting Palm: The Inside Story of Palm, Handspring, and the Birth of the Billion-Dollar Handheld Industry*. New York: John Wiley and Sons, 2002.

Campbell, Joseph. *The Power of Myth*. With Bill Moyers. Edited by Betty Sue Flowers. 1988. Reprinted, New York: Anchor Books, 1991.

Chislenko, Alexander. "Automated Collaborative Filtering and Semantic
    Transports." *Home and Neighborhood of Alexander (Sasha) Chislenko*,
    15 October 1997, Version 0.72.
    http://www.lucifer.com/~sasha/articles/ACF.html (20 September 2004).

Christophe, Véronique, and Bernard Rimé. "Exposure to the social sharing of
    emotion: Emotional impact, listener responses and secondary sharing."
    *European Journal of Social Psychology* 27, no. 1 (1997): 37-54.

Cohen, Bernard C. *The Press and Foreign Policy*. Princeton, NJ: Princeton
    University Press, 1963.

Corballis, Michael C. "A gesture in the right direction?" *Brain and Behavioral
    Sciences* 16, no. 4 (1993): 697.

_____. *From Hand to Mouth: The Origins of Language*. Princeton, NJ:
    Princeton University Press, 2002.

Crowley, Mike, and Melanie Crowley. *Take Our Word For It*, no. 50 (August 16,
    1999). http://www.takeourword.com/Issue050.html
    (September 13, 2004).

Denton, Nick. "Second Sight: The atrocity through the eyes of weblogs."
    *Guardian Unlimited*, September 20, 2001.
    http://www.guardian.co.uk/Archive/Article/ 0,4273,4260486,00.html.

Derbaix, Christian and Joëlle Vanhamme. "Inducing word-of-mouth by eliciting
    surprise – a pilot investigation." *Journal of Economic Psychology* 24,
    no. 1 (2003): 99-116.

Drezner, Daniel W., and Henry Farrell. "Web of Influence." In B*log! How the
    Newest Media Revolution Is Changing Politics, Business, and Culture*,
    edited by David Kline and Dan Burstein, 82-97. New York: CDS Books,
    2005.

Dubrovsky, Vitaly J., Sara Kiesler, and Beheruz N. Sethna. "The Equalization
    Phenomenon: Status Effects in Computer-Mediated and Face-to-Face
    Decision Making Groups." *Human-Computer Interactions* 6, no. 2
    (1991): 119-146.

"Ericsson CEO sees global mobile phone users at 3 bln next yr vs current 2.2 bln."
    *Forbes.com*, September 09, 2006.
    http://www.forbes.com/business/feeds/afx/2006/09/06/afx2998665.html
    (December 04, 2006).

"Federal Communications Commission Releases Data On High-Speed Services For
    Internet Access." *Federal Communications Commission*, July 26, 2006.
    http://hraunfoss.fcc.gov/edocs_public/attachmatch/DOC-266593A1.pdf.

Dunbar, Robin I. M. "Coevolution of neocortical size, group size and language in humans." *Behavioral and Brain Sciences* 16, no. 4 (1993): 681-735.

_____. *Grooming, Gossip, and the Evolution of Language.* Cambridge, MA: Harvard University Press, 1996.

Fox, Maggie. "Deaf children reveal how language is born: Study in Nicaragua traces development of new signs." *MSNBC.com*, September 17, 2004. http://msnbc.msn .com/id/6029190/ (October 10, 2004).

Gardner, R.A., and B.T. Gardner. "Teaching Sign Language to a Chimpanzee." *Science* 165, no. 3894 (1969): 664-672.

Gendron, George, and Bo Burlingham. "The Entrepreneur of the Decade: An Interview with Steve Jobs." *Inc.* 11, no. 4 (1989): 114-128.

Gladwell, Malcolm. *The Tipping Point: How Little Things Can Make A Big Difference.* 2000. Reprinted with a new afteward, NY: Back Bay Books, 2002.

Goetzl, David. "New Data Reveals Virtually No Viewers For Time-Shifted Spots." *MediaDailyNews*, April 06, 2006. http://publications.mediapost.com-/index.cfm?fuseaction=Articles.showArticleHomePage&art_aid=41887 (December 04, 2006).

Goffman, Erving. *The Presentation of Self In Everyday Life.* 1956. Reprinted, NY: Anchor Books, 1959.

Goodman, Robert F. Introduction to *Good Gossip*, edited by Robert F. Goodman and Aaron Ben-Ze'ev, 1-8. Lawrence, KS: University Press of Kansas, 1994.

Govier, Trudy. *Dilemmas of Trust.* Montreal, Canada: McGill-Queen's University Press, 1998.

Granovetter, Mark S. "The Strength of Weak Ties." *American Journal of Sociology* 78, no. 6 (1973): 1360-1380.

Grossman, Lev. "Meet Joe Blog." *Time Magazine* 163, no. 25 (2004): 64-70.

Hargrove, Barbara. "Integrative and Transformative Religions." In *Understanding the New Religions*, edited by Jacob Needleman and George Baker, 257-266. 1978. Reprinted, New York: The Seabury Press, 1981.

Hawkins, David. Truth Vs. Falsehood: How to Tell the Difference. Toronto: Axial Publishing Company, 2005

Higgins, Dennis. *The Art of Writing Advertising: Conversations with Masters of the Craft: David Ogilvy, William Bernbach, Leo Burnett.* 1968. Reprinted, New York: McGraw-Hill, 2003.

"Internet Usage Statistics – The Big Picture: World Internet Users and Population Stats." *Internet World Stats: Usage and Population Statistics*, November 27, 2006. http://www.internetworldstats.com/stats.htm (December 04, 2006).

Hoffer, Eric. *The True Believer: Thoughts on the Nature of Mass Movements.* New York: Harper and Brothers, 1951.

Kamins, Michael A., Valerie S. Folkes, and Lars Perner. "Consumer Responses to Rumors: Good News, Bad News." *Journal of Consumer Psychology* 6, no. 2 (1997):165-187.

Kaplan, Dan. "Enterprises beware: IM attacks break record, again." *SC Magazine UK*, October 31, 2006. http://www.scmagazine.com/uk/news/article/601820/enterprises-beware-im-attacks-break-record-again/.

Kelly, Kevin. "We Are the Web." Wired 13, no. 08 (2005): 92-101.
Kirkpatrick, David, and Daniel Roth. "Why There's No Escaping the Blog." In *Blog! How the Newest Media Revolution Is Changing Politics, Business, and Culture,* edited by David Kline and Dan Burstein, 210-220. New York: CDS Books, 2005.

Kleinfeld, Judith S. "The Small World Problem." *Society* 34, no. 2 (2002): 61-66.

Kline, David. "Toward A More Participant Democracy." In *Blog! How the Newest Media Revolution Is Changing Politics, Business, and Culture,* edited by David Kline and Dan Burstein, 3-24. New York: CDS Books, 2005.

Kurzweil, Ray. "The Law of Accelerating Returns." *KurzweilAI.net,* March 7, 2001. http://www.kurzweilai.net/meme/frame.html?main=/articles/art0134.html (September 08, 2004).

"Lands end is moving its success in online custom clothing to the catalog." *internet retailer*, February 26, 2004. http://www.internetretailer.com/dailyNews.asp?id=11383 (December 04, 2006).

Latourette, Kenneth Scott. *A History of the Expansion of Christianity*, vol. 1, *The First Five Centuries.* New York: Harper and Brothers Publishers, 1937.

Layden, Tim. "Bracelet mania: Armstrong's yellow wrist bands have become cultural phenomenon." *SI.com,* September 10, 2004. http://sportsillustrated.cnn.com/2004/ writers/tim_layden/09/10/layden.0910/index.html (December 06, 2005).

Leavens, David A. and William D. Hopkins. "Intentional Communication by
    Chimpanzees: A Cross-Sectional Study of the use of Referential
    Gestures." *Developmental Psychology* 34, no. 5 (1998): 813-822.

Levin, Steve. "Guarding Your Tongue." *Pittsburgh Post-Gazette*, December 27,
    2000, sec. e.

Levitt, Steven D., and Stephen J. Dubner. *Freakanomics: A Rogue Economist
    Explores the Hidden Side of Everything.* New York: HarperCollins
    Publishers, William Morrow, 2005.

Lieber, Jill. "Brace yourself: Wristbands have become the latest fundraising and
    fashion trend." *USA Today*, December 05, 2005, sec. c.

Lumley, Frederick Elmore. *Means of Social Control.* New York:
    The Century, 1925.

Mackay, Charles. *Extraordinary Popular Delusions and the Madness of Crowds.*
    1841. Reprinted with a facsimile of the title pages and reproductions of
    original illustrations from the 1841 and 1852 editions with a forward by
    Bernard M. Baruch. New York: Farrar, Straus and Giroux, 1932.

Mann, Charles C. "A Remote Control For Your Life." *MIT's Technology Review*
    107, no. 6 (2004): 42-49.

Maslow, Abraham. *Maslow On Management.* With Deborah C. Stephens and
    Gary Heil. New York: John Wiley and Sons, 1998.

_____. *Motivation and Personality.* 3rd ed. New York: Longman Addison
    Wesley, 1987.

McCoy, Elin. *The Emperor of Wine: The Rise of Robert M. Parker, Jr. and the
    Reign of American Taste.* New York: HarperCollins Publishers, 2005.

McInerney, Jay. *Bacchus & Me: Adventures in the Wine Cellar.* 2000. Reprinted,
    New York: Vintage Books, 2002.

"Messaging." *GSM World.* http://www.gsmworld.com/services/messaging.shtml
    (December 04, 2006).

Milgram, Stanley. "The Small-World Problem." *Psychology Today* 1, no. 1
    (1967):  60-67.

Moore, Robert Laurence. *Religious Outsiders and the Making of Americans.* New
    York: Oxford University Press, 1986.

Mucha, Thomas. "Young and Upwardly Mobile." *Business* 2.0, July 01, 2004.
    http://www.business2.com/b2/web/articles/0,17863,659808,00.html
    (September 12, 2004)

Munoz, Lorenza. "High-Tech Word of Mouth Maims Movies in a Flash." *Los Angeles Times*, August 17, 2003, final ed., sec. a.

Myers, David G. *Intuition: Its Powers and Perils*. New Haven, CT: Yale University Press, 2002.

Neistat, Casey. Interview by Cavuto. *Fox News*. Fox. January 09, 2004.

Neistat, Casey, and Van Neistat. *iPod's Dirty Secret,* 2003. http://www.ipodsdirtysecret .com.

Nicholson, Nigel. "The new word on GOSSIP." *Psychology Today* 34, no. 3 (2001): 40-45.

Nogueira, Paulo. "Site posts low-tech hack for iTunes giveaway." *CNN.com*, February 20, 2004. http://www.cnn.com/2004/TECH/internet/02/19/pepsi.itunes.promo tion/ (September 09, 2004).

Pandya, Gitesh. *Box Office Guru*. http://www.boxofficeguru.com (December 06, 2005).

Pink, Daniel H. "The Book Stops Here." *Wired* 13, no. 03 (2005):124-129, 136, 139.

Pinker, Steven. *The Language Instinct*. New York: William Morrow and Company, 1994.

"Playing the Rating Game." *The Economist* 352, no. 8137 (1999): 94, 96.

Potts, Wayne K. "The chorus line hypothesis of maneuver coordination in avian flocks." *Nature* 309, no. 5966 (1984): 344-345

Prus, Robert C., and C. R. D. Sharper. *Road Hustler: Grifting, Magic, and the Thief Subculture*. 1977. Reprinted and expanded, New York: Richard Kaufman and Alan Greenberg, 1991.

Rhiengold, Howard. *The Virtual Community: Homesteading on the Electronic Frontier*. Reading: Addison-Wesley Publishing Company, 1993.

Roloff, Michael E. "Interpersonal Influence: The View From Between People." In *Communication and Social Influence Processes*, edited by Charles R. Berger and Michael Burgoon, 115-131. East Lansing, MI: Michigan State University Press, 1995.

Rose, Frank. "The Lost Boys." *Wired* 12, no. 08 (2004): 114-119.

Rosen, Emanuel. *The Anatomy of Buzz: How To Create Word-of-Mouth Marketing.* New York: Doubleday, Currency, 2000.

Ruibal, Sal. "Livestrong shows solidarity of 50M." *USA Today,* May 13, 2005, sec. a.

Scoble, Robert. "Blogs: Humanizing the Face of Corporate America." In *Blog! How the Newest Media Revolution Is Changing Politics, Business, and Culture,* interviewed and edited by David Kline and Andrew Burstein, 124-135. New York: CDS Books, 2005.

Smith, John Maynard, and Eörs Szathmáry. *The Majors Transitions in Evolution.* 1995, Reprinted, New York: Oxford University Press, 1997.

Standage, Tom. *The Victorian Internet: The Remarkable Story of the Telegraph and the Nineteenth Century's On-line Pioneers.* New York: Walker Publishing Company, 1998.

"Stephen Hawking: … communicating." *Connected Earth.* http://www.connectedearth.co.uk/Galleries/Itpaystoadvertise/ Thenewage/Pumpingupthevolume/ StephenHawking/index.htm (December 06, 2005).

Steuver, Hank. "Battery and Assault – When His iPod Died, This Music Lover Tackled Apple. Stay Tuned." *The Washington Post,* December 20, 2003, sec. c.

Surowiecki, James. *The Wisdom of Crowds: Why the Many Are Smarter Than the Few and How Collective Wisdom Shapes Business, Economics, Societies and Nations.* New York: Doubleday, 2004.

Tapscott, Don. Growing Up Digital: *The Rise of the Net Generation.* New York: McGraw-Hill, 1998.

Tchong, Michael. *Trendscape* 2004. San Francisco, CA: Trendscape, 2003. Technorati. http://www.technorati.com (June 30, 2006).

*Technorati.* http://www.technorati.com (December 03, 2006)

Travers, Jeffrey, and Stanley Milgram. "An Experimental Study of the Small World Problem." *Sociometry: A Journal of Research in Social Psychology* 32, no. 4 (1969): 425-443.

"U.S. Teens Graduate From Choosing IM Buddy Icons To Creating Elaborate Social Networking Profiles, According to Nielsen//NetRatings." *Nielsen//NetRatings,* October 11, 2006. http://www.netratings.com/press.jsp?section=new_pr&theyear=2006 &country=United%20States&themonth=9.

Walker, Rob. "Yellow Fever." *The New York Times Magazine,*
     August 20, 2004, 23.

Watts, Duncan J. *Six Degrees: The Science of a Connected Age.* New York: W.W.
     Norton and Company, 2003.

Werner, Carol and Pat Parmelee. "Similarity of Activity Preferences Among
     Friends: Those Who Play Together Stay Together." *Social Psychology
     Quarterly* 42, no. 1 (1979): 62-66.

Westen, Robin. "The Real Slant on Gossip." *Psychology Today* 29, no. 4 (1996):
     44-48, 80-81.

"Where's Debbie?: How Consumers Influence Each Other and Practical Steps
     Brands Can Take to Understand and Harness Word of Mouth."
     *Mediaedge:cia*, April 2004.
     http://www.mecglobal.com/output/Page1325.asp.

Witzel, Morgen. "Marketing." *Thoemmes Continuum: The History of Ideas,*
     2000. http://www.thoemmes.com/economics/marketing_intro.htm
     (September 12, 2004).

Zyman, Sergio. *The End of Advertising As We Know It.* Hoboken: John Wiley
     and Sons, 2002.

_____. *The End of Marketing As We Know It.* New York: HarperCollins
     Publishers, 1999.

# ACKNOWLEDGEMENTS

This book can boast many authors; so many souls have journeyed with me to uncover the drivers behind communication. In Nonbox Consulting, our Consumer Insight Think Tank, we use the concept of the "collective hive" to describe the synergistic energy the group creates that helps our ideas evolve. *Why We Talk* is no exception. The collective group effort of our team—Melissa, Salim, Ozzie, Joe, Joze, Aaron, Bill, and Scott—cannot be overstated.

To the co-authors of this book, Bill Eisner, Aaron Shields, and Scott Jeffrey, your contributions are immeasurable.

To my brother Salim for being the initial sounding board and catalyst for the development of this project.

To Rex Williams for the inspiration to explore the topic of *why we talk*.

To Misty Williams for her exceptional editorial and word-crafting abilities.

To Melissa Thornton for her creative brilliance with both the cover and interior design.

To Randy Curtis, Todd Alexander, and Scott Lynch for continually offering fresh insights and perspectives as the work unfolded.

To mom for always believing in me.

To God for guidance, direction, and creativity.

# ABOUT THE AUTHORS

Nonbox Consulting is a collective; a group of inter-connected minds aligned with single purpose: To help you build trust with your customers. From dropouts to biologists, artists to programmers, thinkers to dreamers, each member has his or her own area of expertise, knowledge, and unique perspective on the world. We don't just acknowledge our differences—we celebrate them and capitalize on them! Each individual enhances the collective. And as a collective mind, we serve our customers.

## The "Collective Mind" for *Why We Talk*

**BOLIVAR J. BUENO (BJ)** is in an elite class of thought leaders as a dynamic young lecturer and creative strategist, with interviews by CNN, *USA Today*, *New York Times*, and CNN en Español. BJ is the co-author of *The Power of Cult Branding* (Crown 2002), a work which received rave reviews from leading mavens like Jack Trout, Al Reis, and Jay Conrad Levinson. As a board member of the Retail Advertising & Marketing Association (RAMA) and a member of the Chief Marketing Officers board for international retailers, BJ advises companies like Target, Wal-Mart, Washington Mutual, Toys-R-Us, and JCPenney in their retail, advertising, and marketing efforts. BJ operates Nonbox Consulting based in Orlando, Florida.

Talk with BJ at bjbueno@nonboxconsulting.com.

**BILL EISNER** is a veteran in the communications business with clients like Kohl's Department Stores, 76 Brand Gasoline, Coca-Cola, Miller Beer, and Harley-Davidson. He is the past president of what is now called Intermarket Agency Network and currently serves as faculty and board member for the Retail Advertising and Marketing Association. He is a consultant to the Retail Marketing Institute and is on the Board of Directors of The Eisner Museum of Advertising and Design. Bill is a past board member of the American Advertising

Museum, The Milwaukee Public Museum, and was named to the Board of Governors for The Medill School of Journalism at Northwestern University. Bill co-founded Nonbox with Steve Karakas in 1999.

Talk with Bill at bille@nonbox.com.

**SCOTT JEFFREY** works alongside BJ Bueno as a leading thinker, writer, and partner in Nonbox Consulting. Prior to joining Nonbox, Scott was the master strategist behind Creative Crayon, a world-class strategic coaching enterprise and consultancy. Scott is renowned for uncanny ability to discern the most significant strategic moves to build momentum for his clients toward their ultimate results. He is the author of *Journey to the Impossible: Designing an Extraordinary Life*, a Benjamin Franklin Award finalist. Scott graduated from the University of Michigan.

Talk with Scott at scott@nonboxconsulting.com.

**AARON SHIELDS** is Nonbox Consulting's resident researcher, biologist, integral thinker, and accomplished magician. Aaron brings an unusual mind and idea-producing element to Nonbox, spending his time conducting extensive research through a multidisciplinary approach on topics ranging from advanced theoretical sciences to consumer loyalty programs. Aaron worked as a researcher for the medical director of liver transplant / director of hepatology and for the head of consultation psychiatry at the Hospital of the University of Pennsylvania. He studied Linklater acting/voice technique and performed in Edinburgh, Scotland at the Edinburgh Fringe Festival in 2003. He graduated from the University of Pennsylvania with a B.A. in biology and theater.

Talk with Aaron at aaron@nonboxconsulting.com.

# ABOUT NONBOX CONSULTING

## What do we know?

We know people want to feel free so they can dance. They hit the road all weekend long trying to live freely. We know people want to put on their Spock ears and leave this planet. They told us so. The experience of feeling alive—that's what they want. That's what we know.

Our teachers speak to us through their work and invigorate us to search, to question, to dream. Our journey has only started. Ahead is a long path to an unknown destination. It's *outward* in appearance, *inward* in experience. The more we try to understand ours brothers and sisters, the more we understand ourselves.

"We have not even to risk the adventure alone, for the heroes of all time have gone before us. The labyrinth is thoroughly known. We have only to follow the thread of the hero's path, and where we had thought to find an abomination, we shall find a god. And where we had thought to slay another, we shall slay ourselves. Where we had thought to travel outward, we will come to the center of our own existence. And where we had thought to be alone, we will be with all the world."

–Joseph Campbell

These words inspire us to chase our dreams. That's what we know.

## What do we do?

Our job is to create an environment where your customers want to buy from you (on their terms)—not an environment to sell your wares. When the customer wins, the business wins. It's that simple. We borrow from a wide range of disciplines to help you better understand your customers—psychology, neuroscience, quantum mechanics, consciousness research, philosophy, and mythology—anything that serves us in helping you move your adventure forward. Our teachers include Jung, Freud, Maslow, Hawkins, Sheldrake, Pavlov, Mamet, and Campbell. Through their discoveries, we strive to provide new meaning to the term "consumer insight."

The answers may vary, but the perspective never changes: We must put the customer first and speak about what is relevant to them. We help you connect with your customer. Although our process is highly organic and (at times) unconventional, our results speak for themselves.

# THE NATURE OF TALK
### www.WhyWeTalk.com

# OTHER PUBLICATIONS

Other publications by B.J. Bueno and Nonbox Consulting:

**THE POWER OF CULT BRANDING** (Crown Business, 2002)
*How 9 Magnetic Brands Turned Customers Into Loyal Followers*
*(and Yours Can, Too)*
Coauthored by B.J. Bueno

The groundbreaking book that received rave reviews from leading mavens like Jack Trout, Al Reis, Jay Conrad Levinson, and Jeffrey Fox.

**CULT BRANDING WORKBOOK** (November 2006)
*A Marketer's Guide to Building Customer Loyalty*
B.J. Bueno

A marketer's practical step-by-step guide for building brand loyalty by understanding the basic human needs of their customer and developing a strategy around your "Brand Lovers."

**THE HUMAN INSIGHT READER**
*A Nonbox Consulting Publication*

We periodically publish a series of thoughtful, well-researched papers on various topics that help better understand complex human issues.

**Get More Insight at NonboxConsulting.com**